# First World War
## and Army of Occupation
# War Diary
## France, Belgium and Germany

62 DIVISION
Divisional Troops
Royal Army Service Corps
Divisional Train (525, 526, 527, 528 Companies ASC)
8 January 1917 - 12 August 1919

WO95/3078/5

The Naval & Military Press Ltd
www.nmarchive.com
**Published in association with The National Archives**

Published by

## The Naval & Military Press Ltd

Unit 10 Ridgewood Industrial Park,

Uckfield, East Sussex,

TN22 5QE England

Tel: +44 (0) 1825 749494

www.naval-military-press.com

www.nmarchive.com

*This diary has been reprinted in facsimile from the original. Any imperfections are inevitably reproduced and the quality may fall short of modern type and cartographic standards.*

**© Crown Copyright**
**Images reproduced by permission of The National Archives, London, England, 2015.**

# Contents

| Document type | Place/Title | Date From | Date To |
|---|---|---|---|
| Heading | WO95/3078/5 | | |
| Heading | 62nd Division 62nd Divisional Train ASC Jan 1917 To 1919 Aug | | |
| Heading | War Diary of The 62nd Divisional Train From 1st Jany 1917 To 31st Jany 1917 Volume I | | |
| War Diary | Northampton | 08/01/1917 | 08/01/1917 |
| War Diary | Havre | 09/01/1917 | 10/01/1917 |
| War Diary | Abbeville | 11/01/1917 | 11/01/1917 |
| War Diary | Frohen | 12/01/1917 | 21/01/1917 |
| War Diary | Authieule | 22/01/1917 | 22/01/1917 |
| War Diary | Bus Les Artois | 23/01/1917 | 28/01/1917 |
| War Diary | Bus | 29/01/1917 | 31/01/1917 |
| Heading | War Diary of The 62nd Divisional Train From 1st Feby 1917 To 28th Feby 1917 Volume 2 | | |
| War Diary | Bus Les Artois | 01/02/1917 | 20/02/1917 |
| War Diary | Lealvillers | 21/02/1917 | 28/02/1917 |
| Heading | War Diary of The 62nd Divisional Train From March 1st 1917 To March 31st 1917 Volume 3 | | |
| War Diary | Lealvillers | 01/03/1917 | 06/03/1917 |
| War Diary | Englebelmer | 07/03/1917 | 31/03/1917 |
| Heading | War Diary of The 62nd Divisional Train From April 1st 1917 To April 30th 1917 Volume No 4 | | |
| War Diary | Englebelmer | 01/04/1917 | 03/04/1917 |
| War Diary | Achiet-Le-Grand | 04/04/1917 | 11/04/1917 |
| War Diary | Achiet | 12/04/1917 | 30/04/1917 |
| Heading | War Diary of The 62nd Divisional Train From 1-5-17 To 31-5-17 Volume 5 | | |
| War Diary | Achiet-Le-Grand | 01/05/1917 | 29/05/1917 |
| Heading | War Diary of The 62nd Divisional Train From June 1st 1917 To June 30th 1917 Volume 6 | | |
| War Diary | Achiet-Le-Grand | 02/06/1917 | 28/06/1917 |
| War Diary | Bapaume | 29/06/1917 | 30/06/1917 |
| War Diary | Achiet Le Grand | 25/06/1917 | 29/06/1917 |
| Heading | War Diary of The 62nd Divisional Train From 1st July 1917 To 31st July 1917 Volume 7 | | |
| War Diary | Bapaume | 01/07/1917 | 31/07/1917 |
| Heading | War Diary of The 62nd Divisional From 1st August 1917 To 31st August 1917 Volume 8 | | |
| War Diary | Bapaume | 01/08/1917 | 31/08/1917 |
| Heading | War Diary of The 62nd Divisional Train From 1-9-17 To 30-9-17 Volume 9 | | |
| War Diary | Bapaume | 01/09/1917 | 30/09/1917 |
| Heading | War Diary of 62nd Divisional From 1st October 1917 To 31st October 1917 Volume No 10 | | |
| War Diary | Bapaume | 01/10/1917 | 12/10/1917 |
| War Diary | Rocquigny | 13/10/1917 | 30/10/1917 |
| War Diary | Monchiet | 31/10/1917 | 14/11/1917 |
| War Diary | Rocquigny | 15/11/1917 | 15/11/1917 |
| War Diary | Monchiet | 31/10/1917 | 31/10/1917 |

| | | | |
|---|---|---|---|
| Heading | War Diary of 62nd Divisional Train From Nov 1st 1917 To Nov 30th 1917 Volume XI | | |
| War Diary | Monchiet | 01/11/1917 | 14/11/1917 |
| War Diary | Rocquigny | 15/11/1917 | 17/11/1917 |
| War Diary | Bus | 18/11/1917 | 30/11/1917 |
| Heading | War Diary of 62nd Divisional Train From 1-12-17 To 31-12-17 Volume 12 | | |
| War Diary | Bus | 01/12/1917 | 04/12/1917 |
| War Diary | Monchiet | 05/12/1917 | 06/12/1917 |
| War Diary | Savy | 07/12/1917 | 12/12/1917 |
| War Diary | St Sauveur | 13/12/1917 | 16/12/1917 |
| War Diary | Bas Rieux | 17/12/1917 | 19/12/1917 |
| War Diary | Savy | 20/12/1917 | 31/12/1917 |
| War Diary | Bapaume | 01/07/1917 | 12/10/1917 |
| War Diary | Rocquigny | 13/10/1917 | 17/11/1917 |
| War Diary | Bus | 20/11/1917 | 04/12/1917 |
| War Diary | Monchiet | 05/12/1917 | 06/12/1917 |
| War Diary | Savy | 07/12/1917 | 12/12/1917 |
| War Diary | St Sanveur | 13/12/1917 | 16/12/1917 |
| War Diary | Bus Rioux | 18/12/1917 | 19/12/1917 |
| War Diary | Savy | 20/12/1917 | 30/12/1917 |
| Heading | War Diary of 62nd Divisional Train From Jany 1st 1918 To Jany 31st 1918 Volume 13 | | |
| War Diary | Savy | 01/01/1918 | 12/01/1918 |
| War Diary | Madagascar | 13/01/1918 | 31/01/1918 |
| Heading | War Diary of 62nd Divisional Train From February 1st To February 28th 1918 Volume 14 | | |
| War Diary | Madagascar | 01/02/1918 | 10/02/1918 |
| War Diary | Mingoval | 11/02/1918 | 28/02/1918 |
| Heading | War Diary of 62nd Divisional Train From March 1st 1918 To March 31st 1918 Volume 15 | | |
| War Diary | Mingoval | 01/03/1918 | 04/03/1918 |
| War Diary | Ecurie | 05/03/1918 | 24/03/1918 |
| War Diary | Berneville | 25/03/1918 | 25/03/1918 |
| War Diary | Fonquevillers | 26/03/1918 | 27/03/1918 |
| War Diary | Humbercamp | 28/03/1918 | 31/03/1918 |
| Heading | War Diary of 62nd Divisional Train From 1st April 1918 To 30th April 1918 Volume 16 | | |
| War Diary | Pas | 01/04/1918 | 07/04/1918 |
| War Diary | Henu | 08/04/1918 | 17/04/1918 |
| War Diary | Pas | 18/04/1918 | 30/04/1918 |
| Heading | War Diary of 62nd Divisional Train From 1st May 1918 To 31st May 1918 Volume 17 | | |
| War Diary | Pas | 01/05/1918 | 31/05/1918 |
| Heading | War Diary of 62nd Divisional Train Volume No.18 From 1st June 1918 To 30th June 1918 | | |
| War Diary | Pas | 01/06/1918 | 30/06/1918 |
| Heading | War Diary of 62nd Divisional Train From July 1st 1918 To July 31st 1918 Volume 19 | | |
| War Diary | Pas | 01/07/1918 | 19/07/1918 |
| War Diary | Foret De Reims | 20/07/1918 | 31/07/1918 |
| Heading | War Diary of 62nd Divisional Train From 1st August 1918 To 31st August 1918 Volume 20 | | |
| War Diary | Plivot | 01/08/1918 | 04/08/1918 |
| War Diary | Pas | 05/08/1918 | 16/08/1918 |
| War Diary | Authie | 17/08/1918 | 19/08/1918 |

| | | | |
|---|---|---|---|
| War Diary | Pas | 20/09/1918 | 21/09/1918 |
| War Diary | Orville | 22/08/1918 | 22/08/1918 |
| War Diary | Pas | 23/08/1918 | 25/08/1918 |
| War Diary | Bienvillers | 26/08/1918 | 31/08/1918 |
| Heading | War Diary of 62nd Divisional Train From 1.9.18 to. 30.9.18. Volume. 21. | | |
| War Diary | Courcelles | 01/09/1918 | 10/09/1918 |
| War Diary | Haplincourt | 11/09/1918 | 14/09/1918 |
| War Diary | Courcelles | 15/09/1918 | 25/09/1918 |
| War Diary | Beaumetz | 26/09/1918 | 29/09/1918 |
| War Diary | Havrincourt | 30/09/1918 | 30/09/1918 |
| Heading | War Diary of 62nd Divisional Train From 1.10.18. to 31.10.18 Volume. 22. | | |
| War Diary | Havrincourt | 01/10/1918 | 12/10/1918 |
| War Diary | Cattanieres | 13/10/1918 | 19/10/1918 |
| War Diary | Bevillers | 20/10/1918 | 31/10/1918 |
| Heading | War Diary of 62nd Divisional Train From 1.11.18 to 30.11.18. Volume. 23 | | |
| War Diary | Quievy | 01/11/1918 | 04/11/1918 |
| War Diary | Ruesnes | 05/11/1918 | 08/11/1918 |
| War Diary | Obies | 09/11/1918 | 10/11/1918 |
| War Diary | Neuf-Mesnil | 11/11/1918 | 16/11/1918 |
| War Diary | Sous-Le-Bois | 17/11/1918 | 20/11/1918 |
| War Diary | Somzee | 21/11/1918 | 24/11/1918 |
| War Diary | Denee | 25/11/1918 | 26/11/1918 |
| War Diary | Corbion | 27/11/1918 | 30/11/1918 |
| Heading | War Diary of 62nd Divisional Train From 1.12.18 to. 31.12.18. Volume.24 | | |
| War Diary | Corbion | 01/12/1918 | 11/12/1918 |
| War Diary | Hamoir | 12/12/1918 | 13/12/1918 |
| War Diary | Vielsalm | 14/12/1918 | 16/12/1918 |
| War Diary | Malmedy | 17/12/1918 | 21/12/1918 |
| War Diary | Schleiden | 22/12/1918 | 31/12/1918 |
| Heading | War Diary of 62nd Divisional Train From. 1.1.19. to. 31.1.19. Volume 25. | | |
| War Diary | Schleiden | 01/01/1919 | 31/01/1919 |
| Heading | War Diary of 62nd Divisional Train From 1.2.18. to 28.2.18 Volume 26. | | |
| War Diary | Schleiden | 01/02/1919 | 28/02/1919 |
| Heading | War Diary of Highland Divisional Train From 1st March 1919 To 31st March 1919. Volume 26 | | |
| War Diary | Schleiden | 01/03/1919 | 24/03/1919 |
| War Diary | Duren | 25/03/1919 | 30/04/1919 |
| Heading | War Diary of Highland Divisional Train From 1st May 1919 To 31st May 1919 | | |
| War Diary | Duren | 01/05/1919 | 31/07/1919 |
| Heading | War Diary of Highland Divisional Train From August 1st 1919 To August 12th 1919 | | |
| War Diary | Duren | 01/08/1919 | 11/08/1919 |
| War Diary | On Rail | 11/08/1919 | 11/08/1919 |
| War Diary | Calais | 12/08/1919 | 12/08/1919 |

M0951 3078/5 15909

## 62ND DIVISION

### 62ND DIVISIONAL TRAIN A.S.C.

JAN 1917-~~DEC 1919~~

1919 AUG

525 - 528 Coys ASC

62ND DIVISIONAL TRAIN A.S.C.

ORIGINAL        CONFIDENTIAL

Vol I

War Diary
of
The 62nd Divisional Train

from
1st Jany 1917 to 31st Jany 1917.

Volume I

A.H.Shillinford
Lieut Colonel
Comdg 62nd Divisional Train

Army Form C. 2118.

# WAR DIARY
## of
## INTELLIGENCE SUMMARY.
(Erase heading not required.)

ORIGINAL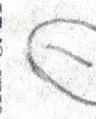

Instructions regarding War Diaries and Intelligence Summaries are contained in F.S. Regs., Part II. and the Staff Manual respectively. Title pages will be prepared in manuscript.

### 62ND DIVISIONAL TRAIN.

| Place | Date | Hour | Summary of Events and Information | Remarks and references to Appendices |
|---|---|---|---|---|
| NORTHAMPTON | 8/11/17 | 9:15AM | Headquarters & 525 Company A.S.C. entrained NORTHAMPTON arrived SOUTHAMPTON 3:45 P.M. Detrained 4:45 P.M. Embarkation completed 6.0 P.M. Sailed 7.0 P.M. on S.S. North West Miller & Suspah. | Nil |
|  |  |  | 526 Company A.S.C. entrained BEDFORD arrived SOUTHAMPTON 2:45 P.M. Embarkation complete 6.0 P.M. Sailed 7.0 P.M. on S.S. North West Miller. Sea rough & wind strong. | Nil |
| HAVRE | 9/1/17 |  | Arrived off HAVRE about 4:30 A.M. Both boats arriving approximately the same time. Entered harbour & berthed about 11 A.M. Disembarkation completed by 4:30 P.M. Headquarters and both companies arrived to Docks Rest Camp HAVRE | Nil |
|  | 10.1.17 |  | 525 & 526 Companies entrained at HAVRE. C.O. & Adjutant proceeded by motor car & reported from A.D.T. Base HAVRE to ABBEVILLE & reported to Advanced Base Commandant at 6 P.M. Snow. | Nil |
|  |  |  | 527 Company A.S.C. entrained at BEDFORD and proceeded to SOUTHAMPTON where they spent the night. | Nil |
| ABBEVILLE | 11.1.17 |  | C.O. & Adjutant proceeded by car for ABBEVILLE to FRANEY-LE-GRAND under orders from Advanced Base Commandant ABBEVILLE & reported at H.Q. 62nd Division at 12:30 P.M. Snow. | Nil |
|  |  |  | 527 Company A.S.C. embarked at SOUTHAMPTON and sailed about 8 P.M. S.S. Archimedes | Nil |

A.F.Wilkinson, Lieut. Col.
Commdg. 62nd Divisional Train.

**Army Form C. 2118.**

ORIGINAL ②

# WAR DIARY
## or
## ~~INTELLIGENCE~~ SUMMARY.
*(Erase heading not required.)*

Instructions regarding War Diaries and Intelligence Summaries are contained in F.S. Regs, Part II. and the Staff Manual respectively. Title pages will be prepared in manuscript.

## 62ND DIVISIONAL TRAIN.

| Place | Date | Hour | Summary of Events and Information | Remarks and references to Appendices |
|---|---|---|---|---|
| FROHEN | 12.1.17 | | 525 Company A.S.C. arrived FREVENT 1 A.M. Detrained and marched to FROHEN arriving at 5 A.M. | APPS |
| | | | 526 Company A.S.C. arrived at BONNIERES at 10 P.M. on 11.1.17 and entrained arrived at 10 A.M. | APPS |
| | | | 527 Company Nº 5 arrived HAVRE and proceeded to Nº 2 Rest Camp HAVRE. 527 Company A.S.C. entrained at WELLINGBOROUGH and proceeded to SOUTHAMPTON & embarked on S.S. Northwestern Miller & arrived at HAVRE. | APPS |
| | 13.1.17 | | 528 Company A.S.C. arrived at HAVRE & proceeded to No 2 Rest Camp | APPS |
| | 14.1.17 | | 527 Company A.S.C. detrained at AUXI-LE-CHATEAU & marched to NOEUX | APPS |
| | | | 528 Company A.S.C. entrained at HAVRE. | APPS |
| | 15.1.17 | | 528 Company A.S.C. detrained at AUXI-LE-CHATEAU & marched to NEUVILLETTE. | |
| | 16.1.17 to 21.1.17 | | Normal Transport Supply Services of the Division. Drawing from BOUQUEMASON by D.S.C. Refilling Points. Divisional Troops — FROHEN - MEZEROLLES - Road<br>185th Brigade Group. BONNIERES - MON LEBLOND<br>186th Brigade Group. NOEUX<br>157th Brigade Group. NEUVILLETTE | APPS |

[signature]
LIEUT. COLONEL,
COMMDG. 62nd DIVISIONAL TRAIN.

Army Form C. 2118.

ORIGINAL (3)

# WAR DIARY
## ~~INTELLIGENCE SUMMARY~~
(Erase heading not required.)

### 62ND DIVISIONAL TRAIN.

| Place | Date | Hour | Summary of Events and Information | Remarks and references to Appendices |
|---|---|---|---|---|
| AUTHIEULE. | 22.1.17 | | Mops Train & 526, 527 & 528 Companies A.S.C. marched to AUTHIEULE. Fighting Train for Athorise Infantry Brigade Groups on DOULLENS – HAUTE VISEE road. Divisional Troops as before. | ATK |
| BUS-LES-ARTOIS | 23.1.17 | | Mops Train & 526, 527 & 528 Companies marched from AUTHIEULE – Mops Train to BUS. 526 Coy to ST LEGER & 527 & 528 Companies to BOIS DU WARNIMONT into huts. Fighting Train to BUS – AUTHIE ROAD. Railhead for Infantry Brigade Groups. BELLE EGLISE. | ATK |
| | | | 525 Coy A.S.C. marched from FROHEN to AUTHIEULE. Supplies drawn by M.T. from BOUQUEMAISON. Refilling Point DOULLENS – HAUTE VISEE Road. Severe frost. | ATK |
| | 24.1.17 | | # 525 Coy A.S.C. marched from AUTHIEULE to BOIS DU WARNIMONT into huts. Railhead for whole Division. BELLE EGLISE – Supplies for whole Division drawn by M.T. Refilling Point for whole Division on BUS-AUTHIE road. Frost continued. | ATK |
| | | | 526 Coy arrived into huts at ST LEGER. 5 SHETS 7.D. Supplies drawn from Railhead by M.T. McD.S.C. having been withdrawn for Corps Transport. | ATK |
| | 25.1.17 | | Loading commenced 10.30 A.M. Frost continued. | |
| | 26.1.17 | | Pack Train arrived Railhead 10 P.M. Refilling time 6.30 – 7.45 A.M. 27.1.17 Frost continued. | ATK |
| | 27.1.17 | | Pack Train arrived Railhead 9.30 P.M. Issued to units from Supply Column Reserve Instructions | ATK |
| | 28.1.17 | | Pack Train arrived Railhead 2 P.M. Issued to units of Supplies drawn from Railhead yesterday. Frost continued. | ATK |

A.H. Williefores.
LIEUT. COLONEL
COMDG. 62ND DIVISIONAL TRAIN.

Army Form C. 2118.

ORIGINAL (4)

# WAR DIARY
## or
## INTELLIGENCE SUMMARY.
*(Erase heading not required.)*

Instructions regarding War Diaries and Intelligence Summaries are contained in F. S. Regs., Part II. and the Staff Manual respectively. Title pages will be prepared in manuscript.

| Place | Date | Hour | Summary of Events and Information | Remarks and references to Appendices |
|---|---|---|---|---|
| | | | 62ND DIVISIONAL TRAIN. | |
| BUS | 29.1.17 | | Pack Train arrived Railhead 4.30 P.M. Refill 9 A.M. Frost continued | ///// |
| | 30.1.17 | | Pack Train arrived Railhead 4.30 P.M. do. | ///// |
| | 31.1.17 | | Pack Train arrived Railhead 12.30 P.M. do. | ///// |

A.J.Phillips Gree
LIEUT. COLONEL,
COMMDG. 62ND DIVISIONAL TRAIN.

CONFIDENTIAL.

ORIGINAL.

WAR DIARY.

of

the 62nd. DIVISIONAL TRAIN.

FROM 1st. FEBY. 1917
TO. 28th. FEBY. 1917

Volume. 2

[signature]
LIEUT. COLONEL.
COMMDG. 62nd DIVISIONAL TRAIN.

Sheet 1

Army Form C. 2118.

# WAR DIARY
## or
## INTELLIGENCE SUMMARY
*(Erase heading not required.)*

ORIGINAL

Instructions regarding War Diaries and Intelligence Summaries are contained in F. S. Regs., Part II. and the Staff Manual respectively. Title pages will be prepared in manuscript.

| Place | Date | Hour | Summary of Events and Information | Remarks and references to Appendices |
|---|---|---|---|---|
| | | | 62ND DIVISIONAL TRAIN. | |
| BUS LES ARTOIS | 1.2.17 | | RAILHEAD — BELLE EGLISE. REFILLING POINTS — BUS-AUTHIE road. | |
| | 2.2.17 | | Pack Train arrived Railhead 9 A.M. Frost continued | HWH |
| | 3.2.17 | | Pack Train arrived Railhead 9 A.M. do | HWH |
| | 4.2.17 | | Pack Train arrived Railhead 11.30 A.M. do | HWH |
| | 5.2.17 | | Pack Train arrived Railhead 9.30 A.M. do | HWH |
| | 6.2.17 | | Pack Train arrived Railhead 9 A.M. do | HWH |
| | 7.2.17 | | Pack Train arrived Railhead 10 A.M. do | HWH |
| | 8.2.17 | | Pack Train arrived Railhead 10.30 A.M. do | HWH |
| | 9.2.17 | | Pack Train arrived Railhead 10.30 A.M. do | HWH |
| | 10.2.17 | | Pack Train arrived Railhead 1 P.M. do | HWH |
| | 11.2.17 | | Pack Train arrived Railhead 6.30 P.M. do | HWH |
| | 12.2.17 | | Pack Train arrived Railhead 10.30 A.M. do | HWH |
| | 13.2.17 | | Pack Train arrived Railhead 4 P.M. do | HWH |
| | 14.2.17 | | Pack Train arrived Railhead 2.30 P.M. do | HWH |
| | 15.2.17 | | Railhead BEAUSSART. Pack Train arrived 8.30 A.M. Frost continued | HWH |
| | | | Pack Train arrived Railhead 12 noon. Frost continued. 527 Company moved to camp at | HWH |

H.W. Phillips
Lieut. Colonel
COMMDG 62ND DIVISIONAL TRAIN

Sheet 2
Army Form C. 2118.
ORIGINAL

# WAR DIARY
or
# INTELLIGENCE SUMMARY.
(Erase heading not required.)

## 62ND DIVISIONAL TRAIN.

| Place | Date | Hour | Summary of Events and Information | Remarks and references to Appendices |
|---|---|---|---|---|
| BUS. LES. ARTOIS. | 15.2.17 (cont'd) | | J.32.b.6.5. (Sheet 57D) taking over from No 3 Company 32nd Divisional Train. | HH6 |
| | 16.2.17. | | Refilling Point for 186th Brigade Group J.27.d.7.7. Pack Train arrived Railhead 7 P.M. Thaw commenced. | HH6 |
| | 17.2.17. | | 526 Company moved to new camp at J.16.d.6.1. and 528 Company to J.26.d.8.3. taking over from Nos. 1 & 4 Companies of 32nd Divisional Train. Pack Train arrived Railhead 10 A.M. Three prisoners escaped from midnight 17/18 Feb. | HH6 |
| | 18.2.17. | | Refilling Point for 185th & 187th Brigade Groups at S.1v J.d.3.3. and T.7.d.5.5. respectively. Pack Train arrived Railhead 5 P.M. Transport worked all through night during Pack Train ~ 120 lbs of coal. | HH6 |
| | 19.2.17. | | 526 Company moved to LEALVILLERS into billets. Pack Train arrived Railhead 11 A.M. | HH6 |
| | 20.2.17. | | 528 Company moved to LEALVILLERS into billets. Pack Train arrived Railhead 8 A.M. | HH6 |
| LEALVILLERS | 21.2.17. | | Hopes Train. 525 Company & 527 Company moved to LEALVILLERS into billets. Pack Train arrived Railhead 11 A.M. Wet weather precautions ordered. | HH6 |
| | 22.2.17. | | Refilling Points for 185th, 186th & 187th Brigade Groups on FORCEVILLE-MAILLY road; for Divisional Troops on LEALVILLERS - LOUVENCOURT road. Pack Train arrived Railhead 8 A.M. | HH6 |
| | 23.2.17. | | Refilling Points for 185th Brigade Group & Divisional Troops in LEALVILLERS village. 186th & 187th | HH6 |

A.J. Phillips
COLONEL.
COMMD. 62ND DIVISIONAL TRAIN.

Sheet 3

Army Form C. 2118.

ORIGINAL

# WAR DIARY
## or
## INTELLIGENCE SUMMARY.
(Erase heading not required.)

Instructions regarding War Diaries and Intelligence Summaries are contained in F. S. Regs, Part II. and the Staff Manual respectively. Title pages will be prepared in manuscript.

| Place | Date | Hour | Summary of Events and Information | Remarks and references to Appendices |
|---|---|---|---|---|
| | | | **62ND DIVISIONAL TRAIN.** | |
| LEALVILLERS | 23.2.17 | (contd) | Brigade Groups as yesterday. Pack Train arrived Railhead 7.30 A.M. | A.F.F.76 |
| | 24.2.17 | | Pack Train arrived Railhead 11 A.M. | A.F.F.76 |
| | 25.2.17 | | RAILHEAD. BELLE EGLISE. Pack Train arrived Railhead 11 A.M. | A.F.F.76 |
| | 26.2.17 | | Refilling Points for 186th & 187th Brigade Groups LEALVILLERS - ACHEUX road. Pack Train arrived Railhead 11.30 A.M. | A.F.F.76 |
| | 27.2.17 | | Pack Train arrived Railhead 4.15 P.M. | A.F.F.76 |
| | 28.2.17 | | Pack Train arrived Railhead 12 noon. | A.F.F.76 |

H.M. Phillips Jones
LIEUT. COLONEL.
COMMDG. 62ND DIVISIONAL TRAIN.

CONFIDENTIAL.

Vol 3

WAR DIARY

OF

THE 62nd DIVISIONAL TRAIN.

FROM :- MARCH 1ST 1917.

TO :- MARCH 31ST 1917.

VOLUME. 3.

ORIGINAL.

[signature]
LIEUT. COLONEL,
COMMDG. 62ND DIVISIONAL TRAIN.

Army Form C. 2118.

ORIGINAL

# WAR DIARY
or
INTELLIGENCE SUMMARY.
(Erase heading not required.)

## 62ND DIVISIONAL TRAIN.

| Place | Date | Hour | Summary of Events and Information | Remarks and references to Appendices |
|---|---|---|---|---|
| LEAVILLERS | 1.3.17 | | RAILHEAD - BELLE EGLISE. Refilling Points - LEAVILLERS - ACHEUX road | |
| | | | Loaded Supplies at Railhead 1 P.M. 186th & 187th Brigade Groups - LEAVILLERS | ATK. |
| | 2.3.17 | | Loaded Supplies at Railhead 1 P.M. 185th Brigade & Divisional Troops Group - LEAVILLERS | |
| | | | 12 G.S. Wagons provided by V Corps to assist with Transport. | ATK. |
| | | | Loaded Supplies at Railhead 1 P.M. 10 G.S. Wagons provided by V Corps to assist with Transport. | ATK. |
| | 3.3.17 | | 8 teams provided by Divisional Artillery. | |
| | | | Loaded Supplies at Railhead 1 P.M. | ATK. |
| | 4.3.17 | | Railhead - VARENNES. Refilling Points 185th Brigade Group & Divisional Troops on VARENNES - ACHEUX road | ATK. |
| | | | 186th & 187th Brigade Groups on LEAVILLERS - ACHEUX road | ATK. |
| | 5.3.17 | | Railhead VARENNES. Refilling Points for all Groups on VARENNES - ACHEUX road | ATK. |
| | 6.3.17 | | do | ATK. |
| ENGLEBELMER | 7.3.17 | | Railhead - AVELUY. Refilling Points unchanged. Train moved to ENGLEBELMER - Headquarters | ATK. |
| | | | Train to Billet No. 6. Four companies on ENGLEBELMER - BOUZINCOURT road in tents. | ATK. |
| | 8.3.17 | | Refilling Points for all Groups on ENGLEBELMER - MAILLY MAILLET road. | ATK. |
| | 9.3.17 | | Refilling Points for all Groups on ENGLEBELMER - AUCHONVILLERS road | ATK. |
| | 10.3.17 | | Refilling Points unchanged. Rationed 14th Army H.A. Brigade who drew supplies direct from Railhead with own Transport. | ATK. |

Signed: [signature]
LIEUT. COLONEL
COMMANDING 62ND DIVISIONAL TRAIN.

Army Form C. 2118.

ORIGINAL

# WAR DIARY
## or
## INTELLIGENCE SUMMARY.
(Erase heading not required.)

## 62ND DIVISIONAL TRAIN.

| Place | Date | Hour | Summary of Events and Information | Remarks and references to Appendices |
|---|---|---|---|---|
| ENGLEBELMER | 11.3.17 | | Railhead & Refilling Points unchanged. Nothing of importance to note. | AFR |
| | 12.3.17 | | Arrangements made to forward supplies for 187th Brigade, D.A.C., 311th Bde R.F.A & 2/1st Field Amb. by rail to HAMEL | AFR |
| | 13.3.17 | | 528 Company moved to HAMEL. Supplies for forward troops sent by rail to HAMEL and dumped at BEAUCOURT at corner of Station Road | AFR |
| | 14.3.17 | | Refilling Point for forward troops at corner of Station Road BEAUCOURT. Other refilling points unchanged. | AFR |
| | 15.3.17 | | Orders 526 Company to move to BEAUCOURT tomorrow in view of a move forward of the 185th Brigade. | AFR |
| | 16.3.17 | | 526 Company moved to BEAUCOURT (R.7.c.). All supplies for 185th Brigade Group, 185th Brigade Group D.A.C. & 311th Brigade R.F.A. sent out by rail to BEAUCOURT, and dumped at corner of Station Road. Supplies for units in back area dumped at ENGLEBELMER - AUCHONVILLERS Road. | AFR |
| | 17.3.17 | | 525 Company moved to R.&A BEAUCOURT - MIRAUMONT road. Received orders at 12.30 A.M. to load up 1 days Iron Rations for Advanced Guard of 2600 all ranks & forage for 2 days for 400 horses to be ready to move at 5.A.M. Later received orders to off load the Iron Rations at BEAUCOURT Dump and the forage rations at Brigade Dump R.H.A. | AFR |
| | 18.3.17 | | | |

W.H.Willoughby Lieut. Colonel
Comdg. 62nd DIVISIONAL TRAIN.

(3)

Army Form C. 2118.

WAR DIARY
or
INTELLIGENCE SUMMARY.
(Erase heading not required.)

ORIGINAL

Instructions regarding War Diaries and Intelligence Summaries are contained in F. S. Regs., Part II. and the Staff Manual respectively. Title pages will be prepared in manuscript.

## 92nd DIVISIONAL TRAIN.

| Place | Date | Hour | Summary of Events and Information | Remarks and references to Appendices |
|---|---|---|---|---|
| ENGLEBELMER | 19.3.17 | | Railhead advanced to BEAUCOURT. 528 Company moved to BEAUCOURT (R.7.c.) Pack Train arrived BEAUCOURT 2:30 p.m. | AH |
| | 20.3.17 | | Road east of BEAUCOURT closed to all traffic supply wagons from 8 A.M. to 2 P.M. considerable difficulty in delivering supplies to units. Arranged to dump supplies for Divisional Troops Group & 186th Brigade units at BOIS D'HOLLANDE dump (R&B.4.p) and to refill for all units in future at 6 A.M. in order to avoid congestion on roads. Arranged for temporary withdrawal of road restrictions for the purpose of delivering supplies. 527 Company moved to ENGLEBELMER – AUCHONVILLERS road. 1 days iron rations + 2 days forage delivered to transport lines of Advanced Guard (2 Infantry Battalions & 1 Battery R.F.A.) drawn from Brigade Dump at R.4.A. | AH |
| | 21.3.17 | | Received orders that supplies for forward troops would be sent by rail tomorrow from BEAUCOURT to MIRAUMONT. Ordered 525 & 526 Companies to prepare to move tomorrow to MIRAUMONT. | AH |
| | 22.3.17 | | 525 Company moved to MIRAUMONT (L.35.A.7.3.) & 526 Company to L.35.c.6.6. Supplies for forward troops arrived at MIRAUMONT at 11 P.M. Considerable difficulty in clearing train owing to congestion in yard & lack of sidings. | AH |

[signature]
Lt. COLONEL.
COMMDG. 92nd DIVISIONAL TRAIN.

Army Form C. 2118.

ORIGINAL

# WAR DIARY
## or
## INTELLIGENCE SUMMARY
*(Erase heading not required.)*

| Place | Date | Hour | Summary of Events and Information | Remarks and references to Appendices |
|---|---|---|---|---|
| | | | **82ND DIVISIONAL TRAIN** | |
| ENGLEBELMER | 23.3.17 | | Refilling Points for Divisional Troops & 186th Brigade Groups at MIRAUMONT stations and for 185th Brigade Group at BOIS D'HOLLANDE dump. | |
| | 24.3.17 | | 2nd Lieut G. Forbes reported for duty & posted to 528 Company. 311th Brigade R.F.A. left the Division accompanied by Train Transport (16 G.S. wagons, 32 H.D. horses & 16 Drivers). Refilling Point for 185th Brigade Group advanced to MIRAUMONT. (R 4 a 8.8.) | |
| | 25.3.17 | | Owing to late arrival of supplies at MIRAUMONT (2.15 A.M) and refusal of French Authorities to allow time for clearing the train fact of the supplies of the 185th Brigade went back on the train to ACHEUX. Arranged to re-consign them to MIRAUMONT with next pack train. | |
| | 26.3.17 | | Indian Cavalry Brigade dumped supplies in Station Yard MIRAUMONT and refilled from these causing congestion & difficulties in forwarding supplies. Made representations to have supplies forwarded from BEAUCOURT to MIRAUMONT by daylight owing to difficulty in off loading in the dark in view of congested state of station yard. | |
| | 27.3.17 28.3.17 | | Supplies sent forward from BEAUCOURT to MIRAUMONT by cart at 12 noon. Same arrangement with regard to supplies as yesterday. Difficulties arose owing to the French Authorities refusing to forward detached trucks from BEAUCOURT to MIRAUMONT. Advised at 10 P.M. that Railhead for tonight refilling would be MIRAUMONT from... | |

LIEUT COLONEL,
82ND DIVISIONAL TRAIN.

Army Form C. 2118.

(5)

WAR DIARY
or
INTELLIGENCE SUMMARY.
(Erase heading not required.)

ORIGINAL

Instructions regarding War Diaries and Intelligence Summaries are contained in F. S. Regs., Part II. and the Staff Manual respectively. Title pages will be prepared in manuscript.

## 52ND DIVISIONAL TRAIN.

| Place | Date | Hour | Summary of Events and Information | Remarks and references to Appendices |
|---|---|---|---|---|
| ENGLEBELMER | 28.3.17 (cont'd) | | to be off loaded & supplies dumped immediately on arrival. | Attd. |
| | 29.3.17 | | Pack Train arrived MIRAUMONT 2:30 A.M. Cleared by 5:30 A.M. and all supplies dumped in Station yard. | Attd. |
| | 30.3.17 | | Refilling Point for 185th & 187th Brigade Groups advanced to MIRAUMONT Goods Station (L.29.D). Two Gunners reported from Base as reinforcements. | Attd. |
| | 31.3.17 | | 10000 Iron Rations and 4000 OXO cubes removed by Motor lorries from dump at Station Rd BEAUCOURT to forward dump at ERVILLERS and dumped at B.19.B.7.5 (Sheet 57c) under a guard. | Attd. |

J.H. Mullinger
LIEUT. COLONEL,
COMMDG. 52ND DIVISIONAL TRAIN.

ORIGINAL.

CONFIDENTIAL.

Vol 4

# WAR DIARY

of

the 62nd Divisional Train

FROM :- April 1st 1917.
TO :- April 30th 1917.

VOLUME No. 4.

Army Form C. 2118.

# WAR DIARY
## or
## INTELLIGENCE SUMMARY.
(Erase heading not required.)

ORIGINAL

Instructions regarding War Diaries and Intelligence Summaries are contained in F. S. Regs., Part II. and the Staff Manual respectively. Title pages will be prepared in manuscript.

| Place | Date | Hour | Summary of Events and Information | Remarks and references to Appendices |
|---|---|---|---|---|
| | | | **62ND DIVISIONAL TRAIN.** | |
| ENGLEBELMER | 1.4.17 | | Applied to D.D.S.T. 5th Army for Rations at ACHIET-LE-GRAND. Informed that it would possibly be available on April 4th. | AAA |
| | 2.4.17 | | Moved 8320 Iron Rations by lorries from BOIS D'HOLLANDE dump to forward dump at ERVILLERS. Provided transport for move of Divisional Headquarters to ACHIET-LE-GRAND. | AAA |
| | 3.4.17 | | Heavy snowstorm in evening. Vans G.S. wagon & (C.T.) attached to Divisional Salvage Officer under orders of V Corps. | AAA / AAA |
| ACHIET-LE-GRAND | 4.4.17 | | Head Qrs. Train & 527 Company moved to ACHIET-LE-GRAND G.4.6. central A.28.d. 9.1 respectively. Railhead ACHIET-LE-GRAND. Train arrived 2.30 p.m. Difficulty in clearing supplies owing to congestion in station yard. | AAA |
| | 5.4.17 | | Refilling Points for all Groups at ACHIET-LE-GRAND - GOMIECOURT ROAD. 525 Company moved to SAPIGNIES H.7.6 central 526 Company to ACHIET-LE-GRAND G.4.6.6.0 and 528 Company to ACHIET-LE-GRAND G.4.6. 7.9. | AAA |
| | 6.4.17 | | Refilling Point for Divisional Troops Group at SAPIGNIES H.7 a 6.5. Remainder unchanged. | AAA |
| | 8.4.17 | | 12 H.D. remount collected by 528 Company from AVELUY. | AAA |
| | 10.4.17 | | Delivered rations to units by Train Transport. Refill at 2.30 p.m. | AAA |
| | 11.4.17 | | Owing to move of Infantry units, rations delivered to them late at night. | AAA |

J M Murphy, LIEUT. COLONEL.
COMMDG. 62ND DIVISIONAL TRAIN.

Army Form C. 2118.

ORIGINAL

# WAR DIARY
## —or—
## INTELLIGENCE SUMMARY.
*(Erase heading not required.)*

Instructions regarding War Diaries and Intelligence Summaries are contained in F. S. Regs., Part II. and the Staff Manual respectively. Title pages will be prepared in manuscript.

## 62ND DIVISIONAL TRAIN

| Place | Date | Hour | Summary of Events and Information | Remarks and references to Appendices |
|---|---|---|---|---|
| ACHIET | 12.4.17 | | Congestion at Railhead owing to replacing of a point north of the station. Great delay in clearing supplies. Received assistance in clearing supplies by 5th Auxtr. lorries. Supplies delivered to units late at night. | |
| | 13.4.17 | | Refilling Points for 186th & 187th Brigade Groups at BIHUCOURT. SAPIGNIES received. Refill 9 A.M. 10 Auxtr. lorries obtained from Div. Supply Column to assist in clearing the pack train. | AJHL |
| | 14.4.17 | | Owing to damage to the Railway track, train was stopped at MIRAUMONT. 22 Auxtr. lorries obtained to assist in clearing the Train. | AJHL |
| | 15.4.17 | | Park Train arrived at ACHIET-LE-GRAND. 10 lorries only available. | AJHL |
| | 19.4.17 | | Infantry units drew supplies from Refilling Points with 1st Line Transport. | AJHL |
| | 20.4.17 | | Refilling Point for Divisional Troops Group moved to H.7 & O.4. | AJHL |
| | 21.4.17 | | Refilling Points for 186th & 187th Brigade Groups moved to H.7 H.1.c.9.5. and H.1.d.o.5. respectively. | AJHL |
| | 22.4.17 | | Conference of Divisional Train Commanders at Office of D.D.S.+T. 5th Army when condition of horses was discussed. Reported 36 H.D. deficient, 27 overworked and 20 sick. Pressed for more regular supply of hay from Army Purchase Board. | AJHL |

M. H. Hughes
LIEUT. COLONEL
COMMDG. 62ND DIVISIONAL TRAIN.

Army Form C. 2118.

# WAR DIARY
## or
## ~~INTELLIGENCE~~ SUMMARY.
*(Erase heading not required.)*

ORIGINAL

Instructions regarding War Diaries and Intelligence Summaries are contained in F. S. Regs., Part II. and the Staff Manual respectively. Title pages will be prepared in manuscript.

### 62ND DIVISIONAL TRAIN

| Place | Date | Hour | Summary of Events and Information | Remarks and references to Appendices |
|---|---|---|---|---|
| ACHIET. | 25.4.17 | | 115 horses attained to unit. AD Transport Supplies from RAILHEAD Inspector of horses by AA & QMG. | Apps. |
| | 26.4.17 | | Asked for 22 lorries for drawing Pack Rations. 15 only available | Apps. |
| | 27.4.17 | | 22 lorries given late for rations work & no horse transport approved. Pack Train arrived 12.30 P.M. Superintendent | Apps. |
| | 28.4.17 | | Inspector of horses of 526, 527 & 578 Companies by DD.ST. 6th Army. | Apps. |
| | 29.4.17 | | Pack Train arrived 1 A.M. | Apps. |
| | 30.4.17 | | Sent 13 men to ABBEVILLE to assist in bringing up Remounts. | Apps. |

H.W. Wilson Jnr.
COMMDG. 62ND DIVISIONAL TRAIN.

ORIGINAL.

CONFIDENTIAL.
Vol 5

WAR DIARY.

OF.

THE 62ND DIVISIONAL TRAIN.

FROM 1-5-17.
TO. 31-5-17.

VOLUME 5.

[signature]
LIEUT. COLONEL,
COMMDG. 62ND DIVISIONAL TRAIN.

Army Form C. 2118.

# WAR DIARY or INTELLIGENCE SUMMARY
*(Erase heading not required.)*

**Original**

Instructions regarding War Diaries and Intelligence Summaries are contained in F.S. Regs., Part II. and the Staff Manual respectively. Title pages will be prepared in manuscript.

## 62nd DIVISIONAL TRAIN.

| Place | Date | Hour | Summary of Events and Information | Remarks and references to Appendices |
|---|---|---|---|---|
| ACHIET-LE-GRAND | 1.5.17 | | Inspection of horses of 526, 527 & 528 Companies A.S.C. by the Divisional Commander. | AWL |
| | 3.5.17 | | Inspected camps of 526 & 528 Companies. | AWL |
| | 4.5.17 | | Received 5 Remounts (R.D.) by road from ABBEVILLE. (1 to 526 Coy, 1 to 527 Company & 3 to 528 Company) | AWL |
| | 5.5.17 | | Inspected camps of 525 & 527 Companies. | AWL |
| | 7.5.17 | | Refilling Point for 187th Brigade Group moved to ACHIET-LE-GRAND – GOMIECOURT road G.4.b.5.8. | AWL |
| | 9.5.17 | | Inspected camp of 527 Company. | AWL |
| | 11.5.17 | | Inspected camps of 525, 526 & 528 Companies. | AWL |
| | 17.5.17 | | Received 15 H.D. remounts from BAPAUME railhead. (7 to 525 Company, 7 to 526 Company & 1 to 527 Company.) | AWL |
| | 21.5.17 | | Refilling Point for 186th Brigade Group moved to ACHIET-LE-GRAND – GOMIECOURT road G.4.b.6.9. | AWL |
| | 22.5.17 | | Received 10 H.D. & 4 R.D. Remounts from BAPAUME railhead – distributed as follows: 4 H.D. & 2 R.D. to 525 Company, 2 H.D. to 526 Company, 2 H.D. & 1 R.D. to 527 Company, 2 H.D. & 1 R.D. to 528 Company. | AWL |

A.M. Mellafont
LIEUT. COLONEL.
COMMDG. 62nd DIVISIONAL TRAIN.

ORIGINAL    Army Form C. 2118.

# WAR DIARY
## or
## INTELLIGENCE SUMMARY.
*(Erase heading not required.)*

| Place | Date | Hour | Summary of Events and Information | Remarks and references to Appendices |
|---|---|---|---|---|
| | | | **62ND DIVISIONAL TRAIN.** | |
| ACHIET-LE-GRAND. | 25.5.17 | | Inspection of Train by Divisional Commander. 4 companies formed up in column of companies in marching order. | MM |
| | 26.5.17 | | Bombs dropped from aeroplanes to N.E. and E. of camp at 10.35 p.m. Shelling by long range enemy gun — objective appeared to be ACHIET railhead. 19 shells fell in vicinity of camp between 10.20 A.M. & 12.10 p.m. Headquarters of Train moved to A.9.6.33. Moved wagon parks + horse lines of 526 Company to W. side of camp | MM |
| | 29.5.17 | | Reinforcement 1 Farrier Staff Sergeant, 1 Saddler & 2 Drivers reported from Base. | MM |

AMKMcInnes
LIEUT. COLONEL
COMMDG. 62ND DIVISION TRAIN

ORIGINAL.

CONFIDENTIAL

9256

War Diary
of
The 62nd Divisional Train

From :- June 1st 1917.
To :- June 30th 1917.

Volume. 6.

A.R.Killinger
LIEUT. COLONEL,
COMMDG. 62ND DIVISIONAL TRAIN.

CONFIDENTIAL

Army Form C. 2118.

ORIGINAL

WAR DIARY
or
INTELLIGENCE SUMMARY.
(Erase heading not required.)

## 62ND DIVISIONAL TRAIN.

| Place | Date | Hour | Summary of Events and Information | Remarks and references to Appendices |
|---|---|---|---|---|
| HEUILLET-LE-GRAND | 2/6/17 | | Remounts collected at BAPAUME station – 1 Charger, 4 Riders 30 H.D. | AMcF. |
| | 3/6/17 | | Remounts distributed to units. 12 H.D. returned by train. One reinforcement reported from Base. | AMcF. |
| | 4/6/17 | | 2 Wagons detailed to convey R.E. material to MORY nightly until further orders for C.R.E. 58th Division. 4 Wagons to 174 Tunnelling Company R.E. to convey stores to ECOUST. | AMcF. |
| | 7/6/17 | | S.Q.M.S. Inkman & Capt. Ratcliffe posted to 42nd Divisional Train for duty. | AMcF. |
| | 8/6/17 | | One reinforcement (C.S.M. Blanagan) reported for A.H.T.Coy. 5th Cavalry Division & posted to 525 Coy. for duty as Acting R.S.M. Seven reinforcements (Drivers) reported for duty from Base. | AMcF. |
| | 10/6/17 | | Twelve men sent to Summer Rest Camp VAIRY-SUR-SOMME. | AMcF. |
| | 11/6/17 | | Thirteen Drivers, 26 horses & 8 G.S. Wagons detached to 119 Labour Company for Hay cutting operations at ERVILLERS & ABLAINZEVILLE. | AMcF. |
| | 12/6/17 | | Remounts (3 Chargers & 2 Riders) collected at BAPAUME station. | AMcF. |
| | 13/6/17 | | Remounts distributed to units. | AMcF. |
| | 14/6/17 | | Instruction of anti-Gas appliances for 526 & 528 Coys under arrangement of D.G.S. | AMcF. |
| | 15/6/17 | | do 527 Coy & Train Hqrs | AMcF. |

AMcF
LIEUT. COLONEL,
COMMDG. 62ND DIVISIONAL TRAIN.

Army Form C. 2118.

ORIGINAL

# WAR DIARY
## or
## INTELLIGENCE SUMMARY.
(Erase heading not required.)

Instructions regarding War Diaries and Intelligence Summaries are contained in F. S. Regs., Part II. and the Staff Manual respectively. Title pages will be prepared in manuscript.

## 62ND DIVISIONAL TRAIN.

| Place | Date | Hour | Summary of Events and Information | Remarks and references to Appendices |
|---|---|---|---|---|
| ACHIET-LE-GRAND | 15/6/17 | | ACHIET-LE-GRAND stables by long range guns | AAA |
| | 16/6/17 | | Details 23 wagons for move of Divisional H.Q. to ACHIET-LE-PETIT. Gas appliances of 525 Coy inspected under arrangement of D.G.O. 2 LD Ambs drawn by 525 Coy from 46th Reserve Park | AAA |
| | 19/6/17 | | Sergt. Pitchforth (526 Coy) posted to S.M.T.O. 7th Corps for duty | AAA |
| | 24/6/17 | | 2 GS wagon limbers for C.R.E. 58th Division cancelled 2 LD carts handed over by 525 Coy to 62nd D.A.C. | AAA |
| | 25/6/17 | | 4 men proceeded to Summer Rest Camp VALERY-SUR-SOMME. 525 Company moved to BAPAUME H 22 C 7.7. (Sheet 57 C) 526 Company moved to BAPAUME H 21 C | AAA |
| | 26/6/17 | | Refilling Point for 185th Brigade Group H 22 C 2.6. (Sheet 57 C) 527 Company moved to BAPAUME H 21 C. | AAA |
| | 27/6/17 | | Refilling Point for Divisional Troops H 22 C 7.1. (Sheet 57 C) Refilling Point for 186th Brigade Group H 21 A 3.4 | AAA |
| | 28/6/17 | | 528 Company moved to BAPAUME H 21 C. | AAA |
| BAPAUME | 29/6/17 | | Refilling Point for 187th Brigade Group H 22 A 3.9 | AAA |

LIEUT. COLONEL,
62nd DIVISIONAL TRAIN.

Army Form C. 2118.

ORIGINAL

# WAR DIARY
## or
## INTELLIGENCE SUMMARY.
(Erase heading not required.)

Summary of Events and Information

### 62ND DIVISIONAL TRAIN.

| Place | Date | Hour | Summary of Events and Information | Remarks and references to Appendices |
|---|---|---|---|---|
| BAPAUME | 29/6/17 | | Train Headquarters moved to BAPAUME. H.21.C.4.4. Sheet 57.C. Divisional Feed Dump & Petrol Dump established at H.22.C.42. RAILHEAD - BAPAUME. Supplies drawn by Horse Transport at 7 A.M. Supplies delivered to units by Train Transport at 9.30 A.M. G.S. Wagons detailed for 194th Tunnelling Company moved at 6 on Battn orders. | JHB |
| | 30/6/17 | | Officer in charge of wagon details for Wagonbury functions (Lieut G. Jones) withdrawn under orders of I Corps. 3 Wagons detailed for 194th Tunnelling Company } details nightly until further orders 4 Wagons for 466 Field Coy R.E. } to carry R.E. material to trenches. Supplies drawn from railhead by Horse Transport at 2 A.M. Refill 7 A.M. by Train Transport. | JHB JHB |

J.H.Whitlow Jones
LIEUT. COLONEL
COMMDG. 62ND DIVISIONAL TRAIN

Army Form C. 2118.

# WAR DIARY
## or
## INTELLIGENCE SUMMARY.
*(Erase heading not required.)*

June

| Place | Date | Hour | Summary of Events and Information | Remarks and references to Appendices |
|---|---|---|---|---|
| ACHIET LE GRAND | 15.6.17 | | 525 Company moved to BAPAUME H.27.c.1.7. (Sheet 57g) | |
| | 16.6.17 | | 576 Company moved to BAPAUME H.7LC. | |
| | 19.6.17 | | 527 Company moved to BAPAUME H.7LC. | |
| | 29.6.17 | | 509 Company moved to BAPAUME H.7LC. | |
| | | | Group shops moved to BAPAUME H.7L.C. & K. | |
| | | | Railhead - BAPAUME. | |

ORIGINAL.

Confidential.

9/61 7

WAR DIARY

of

the 62nd Divisional Train.

from 1st July 1917 to 31st July 1917.

VOLUME 7.

[signature]
LIEUT. COLONEL,
COMMDG. 62ND DIVISIONAL TRAIN.

Army Form C. 2118.

ORIGINAL

# WAR DIARY
## or
## INTELLIGENCE SUMMARY.
*(Erase heading not required.)*

Summary of Events and Information

## 62ND DIVISIONAL TRAIN.

| Place | Date | Hour | Summary of Events and Information | Remarks and references to Appendices |
|---|---|---|---|---|
| BAPAUME. | 1/7/19 |  | Railhead leaving H.T. 7 A.M. |  |
|  |  |  | Following wagons detailed for R.E. services at night. |  |
|  |  |  | 5 to R.E. Dump VAULX 9.30. p.m. |  |
|  |  |  | 2 to 252 Field BEUGNY. 9.0 p.m. |  |
|  |  |  | 6 to 174 Tunnelling Co. BEHAGNIES 8 p.m. | JSJ |
|  | 2/7/19 |  | Gas Alarm received 11.30 p.m. No trace of gas noticed. |  |
|  |  |  | Railhead loading H.T. 4 A.M. |  |
|  |  |  | Transport for R.E. services as on the 1st | JSJ |
|  | 3/7/19 |  | Gas Alarm received 2.30. A.M. No trace of gas noticed. |  |
|  |  |  | Railhead loading H.T. 4 A.M. |  |
|  |  |  | Following wagons detailed for R.E. services at night. |  |
|  |  |  | 4 to R.E. Dump VAULX 9.30 p.m. |  |
|  |  |  | 2 to 252 Field Co. FRAUCOURT 9.0 p.m. |  |
|  |  |  | 6 to 174 Tunnelling Co. BEHAGNIES 8 p.m. |  |
|  | 4/7/19 |  | Railhead loading H.T. 4 A.M. |  |
|  |  |  | 10 wagons to R.E. Dump VAULX at 9.30 p.m. | JSJ |

J.J. Cullen Jones
LIEUT. COLONEL.
COMMDG. 62ND DIVISIONAL TRAIN

Army Form C. 2118.

ORIGINAL

# WAR DIARY
## or
## INTELLIGENCE SUMMARY.
*(Erase heading not required.)*

Instructions regarding War Diaries and Intelligence Summaries are contained in F. S. Regs., Part II. and the Staff Manual respectively. Title pages will be prepared in manuscript.

## 62ND DIVISIONAL TRAIN.

| Place | Date | Hour | Summary of Events and Information | Remarks and references to Appendices |
|---|---|---|---|---|
| BAPAUME | 4.7.17 (contd) | | 6 wagons to 174 Tunnelling Co. BEHAGNIES at 8 p.m. 2 wagons to 252 Field Co. VRAUCOURT at 9 p.m. | |
| | 5.7.17 | | Railhead loading H.T. 7 A.M. Remounts collected from BAPAUME railhead at 10 A.M. 2 chargers, 12 riders. 7 L.D, 3 H.D (1 charger + 5 riders for Train). Transport for R.E. Services as on the 4th. | A.F.1. |
| | 6.7.17 | | Railhead loading H.T. at 7 A.M. Coal Train arrived midday - cleared by H.T. Transport for R.E. Services as on the 4th. | A.F.1. |
| | 7.7.17 | | Railhead loading H.T. at 7 A.M. Transport for R.E. Services as on 4th. 3 O.R. proceeded to Rest Camp VALERY-SUR-SOMME | A.F.1. |
| | 8.7.17 | | Railhead loading H.T. 7 A.M. Transport for R.E. Services as on 4th | A.F.1. |
| | 9.7.17 | | Railhead loading H.T. 7 A.M. Transport for R.E. Services as under. | A.F.1. |

[signature]
LIEUT. COLONEL.
COMMDG. 62ND DIVISIONAL TRAIN

Army Form C. 2118.

ORIGINAL

(3)

# WAR DIARY
## or
## INTELLIGENCE SUMMARY.
(Erase heading not required.)

### 62ND DIVISIONAL TRAIN

| Place | Date | Hour | Summary of Events and Information | Remarks and references to Appendices |
|---|---|---|---|---|
| Bapaume | 9.7.19 | cats | 12 Wagons to R.E. Dump VAULX 9.30 p.m. <br> 6 Wagons to 174 Tunnelling Co BEHAGNIES 6 p.m. <br> 2 Wagons to 252 Field Co VRAUCOURT 9 p.m. <br> 2 Wagons details for 187th Infantry Brigade at 9.15 p.m. returned not required | |
| | 10.7.19 | | Railhead loading H.T. 4 A.M. <br> Transport for R.E. services as on 9th. 1 Reinforcement (C.S.M.) reported. | HSTh. |
| | 11.7.19 | | Railhead loading H.T. 4 A.M. <br> Transport for R.E. services as on 9th | HSTh. |
| | 12.7.19 | | Railhead loading H.T. 7 A.M. <br> Transport for R.E. services as on 9th | HSTh. |
| | 13.7.19 | | Railhead loading H.T. 7 A.M. <br> Transport for R.E. services as on 9th with addition of 2 wagons for 174 Tunnelling Co | HSTh. |
| | 14.7.19 | | Railhead loading H.T. 7 A.M. <br> Transport for R.E. services as under <br> 8 wagons to 174 Tunnelling Co BEHAGNIES 8 p.m. | HSTh. |

H.H.Killer Jones
LIEUT. COLONEL,
COMMDG. 62ND DIVISIONAL TRAIN.

Army Form C. 2118.

ORIGINAL

(4)

# WAR DIARY
## or
## INTELLIGENCE SUMMARY.
(Erase heading not required.)

Instructions regarding War Diaries and Intelligence Summaries are contained in F. S. Regs., Part II. and the Staff Manual respectively. Title pages will be prepared in manuscript.

### 62ND DIVISIONAL TRAIN.

| Place | Date | Hour | Summary of Events and Information | Remarks and references to Appendices |
|---|---|---|---|---|
| BAPAUME | 14.7.17 | cont. | 2 wagons for 461 Field Co. at VAULX at 9.30 p.m. 2 wagons for 452 Field Co. at VRAUCOURT at 9.15 p.m. | ASTS |
|  | 15.7.17 |  | Railhead loading H.T. 4 A.M. Lecture at 6 p.m. on good values by Divisional Agricultural Officer. Transport for R.E Services as on 14th. | ASTS |
|  | 16.7.17 |  | Railhead loading H.T. 4 A.M. Transport for R.E Services as on 14th. | ASTS |
|  | 17.7.17 |  | Railhead loading H.T. 7 A.M. Transport for R.E Services as on 14th. | ASTS |
|  | 18.7.17 |  | Railhead Loading H.T. 4 A.M. Transport for R.E Services as on 14th. 1 Reinforcement (Driver) reported for Base | ASTS |
|  | 19.7.17 |  | Railhead loading H.T. 7 A.M. Coal Train arrived Mid-Day. Cleared by H.T. Transport for R.E Services as on 14.15. | ASTS |

A.F.K.Munford
LIEUT. COLONEL,
COMMDG. 62ND DIVISIONAL TRAIN.

Army Form C. 2118.

ORIGINAL

# WAR DIARY
## or
## INTELLIGENCE SUMMARY.
(Erase heading not required.)

Instructions regarding War Diaries and Intelligence Summaries are contained in F. S. Regs., Part II. and the Staff Manual respectively. Title pages will be prepared in manuscript.

## 62ND DIVISIONAL TRAIN.

| Place | Date | Hour | Summary of Events and Information | Remarks and references to Appendices |
|---|---|---|---|---|
| BAPAUME. | 20.7.17 | 4 A.M. | Railhead loading H.T. 4 A.M. Transport for R.E. services as on 14th except 2 wagons for 252 Field Co. which were cancelled until further orders. Inspected 1st Line Transport of 185th Infantry Brigade. | ASTK |
| | 21.7.17 | 7 A.M. | Railhead loading H.T. 7 A.M. Transport for R.E. services as under. 8 wagons to 174 Tunnelling Co. BEUGNIES. 8 p.m. | ASTK |
| | 22.7.17 | 7 A.M. | Railhead loading H.T. 7 A.M. Transport for R.E. services as on 21st. 1 Officer 7 O.R. proceeded to Rest Camp BEUGNATRE et 9 p.m. VALERY-SUR-SOMME. | ASTK |
| | 23.7.17 | 4 A.M. | Railhead loading H.T. 4 A.M. Inspection of camps of all companies of the Train by Divisional Commander. Transport for R.E. services as on 21st. 12 wagon details for Agricultural Officer at BEUGNATRE at 8.30 p.m. 4 Reinforcements (Drivers) reported from Base. | ASTK |

J.M.Rulling ???
LIEUT. COLONEL.
COMMDG. 62ND DIVISIONAL TRAIN.

Army Form C. 2118.

ORIGINAL

# WAR DIARY
## or
## INTELLIGENCE SUMMARY.
*(Erase heading not required.)*

### 62ND DIVISIONAL TRAIN

| Place | Date | Hour | Summary of Events and Information | Remarks and references to Appendices |
|---|---|---|---|---|
| BAPAUME | 14.7.17 | | Railhead loading H.T. 7 A.M. Transport for R.E. services as under 8 wagons for 174 Tunnelling Company BEHAGNIES 8/m. 2 wagons for 460 Field Co. VAULX 9.30 p.m. | |
| | 25.7.17 | | Railhead loading H.T. 7 A.M. Transport for R.E. services as on 24/7. | |
| | 26.7.17 | | Railhead loading H.T. 4 A.M. Transport for R.E. services as on 24/7. | |
| | 27.7.17 | | Railhead loading H.T. 7 A.M. Transport for R.E. services as under:- 5 wagons for 74 Tunnelling Co. BEHAGNIES 8/m. 2 wagons for 460 Field Co. VAULX 9.30 p.m. | |
| | 28.7.17 | | Railhead loading H.T. 7 A.M. Transport for R.E. services as on 27/7. 6 wagons detailed to report to Agricultural Officer at 3.30 A.M. at BEUGNATRE | |

LIEUT. COLONEL.
COMMDG. 62ND DIVISIONAL TRAIN.

# WAR DIARY or INTELLIGENCE SUMMARY

Army Form C. 2118.

ORIGINAL

## 62ND DIVISIONAL TRAIN

| Place | Date | Hour | Summary of Events and Information | Remarks and references to Appendices |
|---|---|---|---|---|
| BAPAUME | 29.7.17 | 4 A.M. | Railhead loading H.T. 4 A.M. Transport for R.E. services on on 27th. | AAA |
| | 30.7.17 | 4 A.M. | Railhead loading H.T. 4 A.M. Transport for R.E. services as on 27th. | AAA |
| | 31.7.17 | 4 A.M. | Railhead loading H.T. 4 A.M. Transport for R.E. services as under. 5 Wagons for 174 Tunnelling Company BEHAGNIES 8 p.m. 2 Wagons for 460 Field Company VAULX 9.30 p.m. 2 Wagons for 461 Field Company FAVREUIL 8.30 p.m. Lieut. N.B. Lindley proceeded to ENGLAND to report at Officers' Training School at BEDFORD. The Corps Commander inspected the horse lines of all the companies of the Train & expressed his satisfaction with the condition & appearance of the horses. | AAA |

H.H.Billinger
LIEUT. COLONEL.
COMMDG. 62ND DIVISIONAL TRAIN.

Confidential. Vol 8

Original

# WAR DIARY.

of

The 62nd Divisional Train.

from 1st August 1917
to 31st August 1917.

## VOLUME. 8.

[signature]
LIEUT. COLONEL
COMMDG. 62ND DIVISIONAL TRAIN.

Army Form C. 2118.

# WAR DIARY
## or
## INTELLIGENCE SUMMARY.
(Erase heading not required.)

ORIGINAL

### 62ND DIVISIONAL TRAIN.

| Place | Date | Hour | Summary of Events and Information | Remarks and references to Appendices |
|---|---|---|---|---|
| BAPAUME | 1.8.17 | | Railhead BAPAUME. | |
| | | | Refilling Point. Divisional Troops BAPAUME – BEUGNATRE road | |
| | | | 185.186.187 Brigade Groups BAPAUME – FAVREUIL road | |
| | | | Supplies loaded at Railhead on H.T. 4 A.M. | |
| | | | Transport for R.E. services as under:- | |
| | | | 4 Wagons for 178 Travelling Co. 3 p.m. | |
| | | | 2 — 460 Field Co. 8.30 p.m. | |
| | | | 2 — 461 Field Co. 8.30 p.m. | |
| | 2.8.17 | | Railhead loading H.T. 4 A.M. | AP6 |
| | | | Transport for R.E. services as on 1st. | |
| | | | 2 Supplies H.D. horses transferred to 2/1st W.R. Field Ambulance | |
| | | | 1 — 2/1st W.R. Field Ambulance | |
| | 3.8.17 | | Railhead loading H.T. 4 A.M. | AP6 |
| | | | Transport for R.E. services as on 2nd. | |
| | 4.8.17 | | Railhead loading H.T. 7 A.M. | AP6 |
| | | | Transport for R.E. services as on 3rd. | |

A.P. Williams
LIEUT. COLONEL.
COMMDG. 62ND DIVISIONAL TRAIN.

Army Form C. 2118.

# WAR DIARY
## or
## "INTELLIGENCE SUMMARY."
*(Erase heading not required.)*

ORIGINAL

## 62ND DIVISIONAL TRAIN.

| Place | Date | Hour | Summary of Events and Information | Remarks and references to Appendices |
|---|---|---|---|---|
| BAPAUME | 4.8.17 (cont.) | | 2/Lieut A.R. Young reports for duty from HAVRE - posts to 528 Coy. Army ASC. | |
| | | | 5 O.R. reinforcements reported from Base | AAA |
| | | | 4 four horse wagons detailed to report to C.G. Spinal Coy. R.E. at 8 p.m. | |
| | 5.8.17 | | Railhead loading H.T. 7 A.M. | |
| | | | Transport for R.E. services as on 4th with addition of 2 wagons for 174 Tunnelling Co. | AAA |
| | | | 5 four horse wagons detailed to report to G. Spinal Coy. R.E. at 8 p.m. | |
| | 6.8.17 | | Railhead loading H.T. 7 A.M. | |
| | | | Transport for R.E. services as on 5th with addition of 1 wagon for 174 Tunnelling Co. | |
| | | | 5 four horse wagons details to report to G. Spinal Coy. R.E. at 8 p.m. | |
| | | | 3 drivers & 4 H.D. horses detailed for O.C. Haymaking Party EQUILLERS at 10 A.M. | |
| | | | to return after work on 11th | |
| | | | All L.D. & R. horses inspected by VI Corps Horse Management Advisory Officer at | AAA |
| | | | 11 A.M. for selection of lived horses. 3 horses were selected. | |
| | 7.8.17 | | Railhead loading H.T. 7 A.M. | |
| | | | Lieut R. Stenhouse & 2/Lieut J.S. Arkle left 525 Coy. A.S.C. to report to R.F.C. Headquarters | |
| | | | HESDIN. | |

H.A. Milton Owen
LIEUT. COLONEL,
COMMDG. 62ND DIVISIONAL TRAIN.

Army Form C. 2118.

# WAR DIARY
or
INTELLIGENCE SUMMARY.

(Erase heading not required.)

## 62ND DIVISIONAL TRAIN.

| Place | Date | Hour | Summary of Events and Information | Remarks and references to Appendices |
|---|---|---|---|---|
| BAPAUME | 7.8.17 | | Cable Transport for R.E services as under | |
| | | | 2 wagons for 457 Field Co R.E. | |
| | | | 174 Tunnelling Coy. | |
| | 8.8.17 | | Railhead loading H.T. 7 A.M. | Apps. |
| | | | Transport for R.E services as under | |
| | | | 2 wagons for 457 Field Coy R.E. | |
| | | | 2 wagons for 252 " " | |
| | | | 1 wagon for 174 Tunnelling Co | |
| | | | 1 wagon detailed for Divisional boundary nightly until further orders | Apps. |
| | 9.8.17 | | Railhead loading H.T. 7 A.M. | Apps. |
| | | | Transport for R.E services as on 8th | |
| | 10.8.17 | | Railhead loading H.T. 7 A.M. 7th Divisional Artillery attached to our Division for rations | |
| | | | Transport for R.E Services as on 9th | |
| | | | 2/Lieuts R.H Hills & G.F Taylor reported for duty from HAVRE and posted to 525 & 526 Companies respectively. | Apps. |

A.H. Kalenfer
LIEUT. COLONEL.
COMMDG. 62ND DIVISIONAL TRAIN.

Army Form C. 2118.

# WAR DIARY
## or
## INTELLIGENCE SUMMARY.
(Erase heading not required.)

ORIGINAL

### 62ND DIVISIONAL TRAIN.

| Place | Date | Hour | Summary of Events and Information | Remarks and references to Appendices |
|---|---|---|---|---|
| BAPAUME | 11.8.17 | | Railhead loading H.T. 7 A.M. | |
| | | | Transport for R.E services as on 13.8.14 | |
| | | | Coal train cleared by H.T. (16 wagons) | AAG |
| | | | 1 Reinforcement (Farr. S.Sgt.) reported for duty from Base. | AAG |
| | 12.8.17 | | Railhead loading H.T. 7 A.M. | |
| | | | Transport for R.E services as on 11th | |
| | 13.8.17 | | Railhead loading H.T. 7 A.M. | |
| | | | Transport for R.E services as on 12th | |
| | | | 2/Lieut E.A. BURNIE reported for duty from MAURE. Posts & 517 Coy. | AAG |
| | | | 4 O.R. reinforcements reported for duty from Base | |
| | 14.8.17 | | Railhead loading H.T. 7 A.M. | |
| | | | Transport for R.E services as under | |
| | | | 2 wagons for 461 Field Co. R.E. | |
| | | | 7 wagons for 252 Tunnelling Co | AAG |
| | 15.8.17 | | Railhead loading H.T. 7 A.M. | |
| | | | Transport for R.E services as on 14th | AAG |

Lieut. Colonel,
COMMDG. 62ND DIVISIONAL TRAIN.

Army Form C. 2118.

# WAR DIARY
## or
## INTELLIGENCE SUMMARY.
(Erase heading not required.)

ORIGINAL

## 62ND DIVISIONAL TRAIN.

| Place | Date | Hour | Summary of Events and Information | Remarks and references to Appendices |
|---|---|---|---|---|
| BAPAUME | 16.8.17 | | Railhead loading H.T. 7 A.M. Transport for R.E. services as on 15th. | AAA |
| | 17.8.17 | | Railhead loading H.T. 7 A.M. Transport for R.E. services as on 16th. | AAA |
| | 18.8.17 | | Railhead loading H.T. 7 A.M. Transport for R.E. services as on 17th. | AAA |
| | 19.8.17 | | Railhead loading H.T. 7 A.M. Transport for R.E. services as on 18th. | AAA |
| | 20.8.17 | | Railhead loading H.T. 7 A.M. Transport for R.E. services as on 19th. 17 O.R. 24 H.D. horses 12 R. returned from Haymarket Park ERNILLERS. 16 men reported from 252 Employment Company for duty as loaders to replace a similar number of fit Infantry loaders attached. | AAA |
| | 21.8.17 | | Railhead loading H.T. 7 A.M. Transport for R.E. services as on 20th. | AAA |

LIEUT. COLONEL.
COMMDG. 62ND DIVISIONAL TRAIN.

Army Form C. 2118.

ORIGINAL

# WAR DIARY
## or
## INTELLIGENCE SUMMARY.
(Erase heading not required.)

Instructions regarding War Diaries and Intelligence Summaries are contained in F. S. Regs., Part II. and the Staff Manual respectively. Title pages will be prepared in manuscript.

## 62ND DIVISIONAL TRAIN.

| Place | Date | Hour | Summary of Events and Information | Remarks and references to Appendices |
|---|---|---|---|---|
| BAPAUME. | 22.8.17 | 7 A.M. | Railhead loading H.T. 7 A.M. Transport for R.E. services as under 11 wagons for 252 Tunnelling Coy 2 wagons for 461 Field Coy R.E. | |
| | 23.8.17 | 7 A.M. | Railhead loading H.T. 7 A.M. Transport for R.E. services as on 22nd Capt. J. M. Benson M.O. to Train left Kaspot to 7th Division | AAFB |
| | 24.8.17 | 7 A.M. | Railhead loading H.T. 7 A.M. Transport for R.E. services as on 23rd Coal Train cleared by H.T. (16 wagons) | AAFB |
| | 25.8.17 | 7 A.M. | Railhead loading H.T. 7 A.M. Transport for R.E. services as on 24th | AAFB |
| | 26.8.17 | 7 A.M. | Railhead loading H.T. 7 A.M. Transport for R.E. services as on 25th 5 O.R. reinforcements reported for duty from Base | AAFB |

H.H.Mulhern Snr
LIEUT. COLONEL,
COMMDG. 62ND DIVISIONAL TRAIN.

# WAR DIARY
## or
## INTELLIGENCE SUMMARY.
*(Erase heading not required.)*

Army Form C. 2118.

ORIGINAL

### 82ND DIVISIONAL TRAIN.

| Place | Date | Hour | Summary of Events and Information | Remarks and references to Appendices |
|---|---|---|---|---|
| BAPAUME | 27.8.17 | 7 A.M. | Railhead loading H.T. Transport for R.E. services as on 26th. | |
| | 28.8.17 | 7 A.M. | Railhead loading H.T. Transport for R.E. services as on 27th except 2 wagons for 461 Fields Coy which were not required | A.P.B. |
| | 29.8.17 | 7 A.M. | Railhead loading H.T. Transport for R.E. services as under. 11 wagons for 252 Tunnelling Coy 2 wagons for 460 Fields Coy R.E. 8 men attached from 252 Replacement Coy returned to their unit having been classified in Category A. | M.P.S. M.P.S. |
| | 30.8.17 | 7 A.M. | Railhead loading H.T. Transport for R.E. services as on 29th. 2nd Lieut. R.J. Pyke returned for duty from HAVRE Rest to 328 Coy Company | M.P.S. |
| | 31.8.17 | 7 A.M. | Railhead loading H.T. Transport for R.E. services as on 30th. | M.P.S. |

J.A. Mulligan
LIEUT. COLONEL
COMMDG. 82ND DIVISIONAL TRAIN.

Original

Confidential

Vol 9

War Diary
of
the 62nd Divisional Train.
from 1-9-17.
to 30-9-17.

Volume 9.

[signature]
LIEUT. COLONEL.
COMMDG. 62nd DIVISIONAL TRAIN.

Army Form C. 2118.

# WAR DIARY
## or
## INTELLIGENCE SUMMARY.
*(Erase heading not required.)*

ORIGINAL

(1)

## 62ND DIVISIONAL TRAIN.

| Place | Date | Hour | Summary of Events and Information | Remarks and references to Appendices |
|---|---|---|---|---|
| BAPAUME | 1.9.17 | | Railhead BAPAUME. Refilling Points:- Divisional Troops BAPAUME – BEUGNATRE and 185, 186, x187 Brigade Groups BAPAUME – FAVREUIL road. Supplies drawn for Railhead by H.T. 7 A.M. Transport for R.E. services as under:- 11 wagons for 252 Tunnelling Company 2 " " 456 Field Company R.E. 9 Category "B" men reported from 252 Tunnelling Company in relief of 9 Infantry bearers attached. | A/Ph |
| | 2.9.17. | | Railhead loading H.T. 7 A.M. Transport for R.E. services as on 1st. | A/Ph |
| | 3.9.17 | | Railhead loading H.T. 7 A.M. Transport for R.E. services as on 2nd. 3 G.S. wagon details for R.M.R.E. | A/Ph |
| | 4.9.17. | | Railhead loading H.T. 7 A.M. Coal train drawn by 3 G.S. wagons Transport for R.E. services as on 3rd. | A/Ph |

A.H. Butler Grey
LIEUT. COLONEL,
COMMDG. 62ND DIVISIONAL TRAIN.

Army Form C. 2118.

# WAR DIARY
## or
## INTELLIGENCE SUMMARY.
*(Erase heading not required.)*

ORIGINAL (2)

### 62ND DIVISIONAL TRAIN.

| Place | Date | Hour | Summary of Events and Information | Remarks and references to Appendices |
|---|---|---|---|---|
| BAPAUME | 5.9.17 | | Railhead loading H.T. 7 A.M. | AAA |
| | | | Transport for R.E. services as on 4th | |
| | 6.9.17 | | Railhead loading H.T. 7 A.M. | |
| | | | Transport for R.E. Services as on 5th | |
| | | | 4 G.S. Wagons & details for R.M.R.E. | |
| | | | 4 Reinforcements reported for Base Dept. | |
| | | | 2 Lieut. G. Forbes proceeded to Infantry Training School Bolognes | |
| | 7.9.17 | | Railhead loading H.T. 7 A.M. | AAA |
| | | | Transport for R.E. services as on 6th | |
| | 8.9.17 | | Railhead loading H.T. 7 A.M. | AAA |
| | | | Transport for R.E. services as on 7th | |
| | 9.9.17 | | Railhead loading H.T. 7 A.M. | AAA |
| | | | Transport for R.E. services as on 8th | |
| | 10.9.17 | | Railhead loading H.T. 7 A.M. | AAA |
| | | | Transport for R.E. services - 11 wagons for 252 Tunnelling Co. | |
| | | | 3 — 460 Field Co. | |

J.A.K. Hughes
LIEUT. COLONEL,
COMMDG. 62ND DIVISIONAL TRAIN.

Army Form C. 2118.

# WAR DIARY
## or
## INTELLIGENCE SUMMARY.
(Erase heading not required.)

ORIGINAL (3)

## 62ND DIVISIONAL TRAIN.

| Place | Date | Hour | Summary of Events and Information | Remarks and references to Appendices |
|---|---|---|---|---|
| BAPAUME | 10.9.17 | | A Category B clerks reported for HAVRE in relief of 4 Category A clerks. 138 tons of baled hay taken over from VI Corps Hay Office | APP1 |
| | 11.9.17 | | Railheads loading H.T. 7 A.M. Transport for R.E. services as on 10th. | APP2 |
| | 12.9.17 | | Railheads loading H.T. 7 A.M. Transport for R.E. services as on 11th. | APP3 |
| | 13.9.17 | | Railheads loading H.T. 7 A.M. Transport for R.E. services as on 12th. 20 wagons detailed for clearing coal train. | APP4 |
| | 14.9.17 | | Railheads loading H.T. 7 A.M. Transport for R.E. services as on 13th. 2/Lieut. Walsberg's Kan proceeded to report at 11.30p.m. R.F.C. | APP5 |
| | 15.9.17 | | Railheads loading H.T. 7 A.M. Transport for R.E. services as on 14th. | APP6 |
| | 16.9.17 | | Railheads loading H.T. & A.M. Transport for R.E. services as under:- | APP7 |

LIEUT. COLONEL,
COMMDG. 62ND DIVISIONAL TRAIN.

Army Form C. 2118.

# WAR DIARY
## or
## INTELLIGENCE SUMMARY.
(Erase heading not required.)

ORIGINAL (4)

| Place | Date | Hour | Summary of Events and Information | Remarks and references to Appendices |
|---|---|---|---|---|
| BAPAUME | 16.9.17 | | **62ND DIVISIONAL TRAIN.** 11 wagons for 252 Tunnelling Company. 2 wagons for 457 Field Co. R.E. | |
| | 17.9.17. | H.T. 7 A.M. | Dr. Hogan proceeded to Hopu R.F.C. to take up command. Railhead loading. Transport for R.E. services as under:- 5 wagons for 252 Tunnelling Company 2 " " 457 Field Co. " " R.M.R.E. | |
| | | | 4 Category A clerks proceeded to Base. 1 Reinforcement (Sadd S. Bright) reported from 5th Cavalry Reserve Park | |
| | 18.9.17. | H.T. 7 A.M. | Railhead loading. Transport for R.E services as under. 5 Wagons for 252 Tunnelling Company 2 " " 457 Field Co. | |
| | 19.9.17. | H.T. 7 A.M. | Railhead loading. Transport for R.E. services as on 18/9. | |

J.H. Kellner Grant
LIEUT. COLONEL,
COMMDG. 62ND DIVISIONAL TRAIN.

Army Form C. 2118.

ORIGINAL (5)

# WAR DIARY
## or
## INTELLIGENCE SUMMARY

(Erase heading not required.)

Instructions regarding War Diaries and Intelligence Summaries are contained in F.S. Regs., Part II. and the Staff Manual respectively. Title pages will be prepared in manuscript.

## 62ND DIVISIONAL TRAIN.

| Place | Date | Hour | Summary of Events and Information | Remarks and references to Appendices |
|---|---|---|---|---|
| BAPAUME | 20.9.17 | 7 A.M. | Railhead loading H.T. Transport for R.E services as under:- 5 wagons for 252 Tunnelling Co. 4 wagons for 457 Field Co. 4 wagons for R.M.R.E. 2/Lieut C. Brown reported from Base. | AWC |
|  | 21.9.17 | 6 A.M. | Railhead loading H.T. Transport for R.E services as under:- 5 wagons for 252 Tunnelling Co. 2 " " 457 Field Co. Cast horse cleared by 14 G.S wagons | ASC ASC ASC |
|  | 22.9.17 | 6.36 A.M. | Railhead loading H.T. Transport for R.E Services as on 21st. | ASC |
|  | 23.9.17 | 6.30 A.M. | Railhead loading H.T. Transport for R.E services as on 22nd 3 NCOs & 45 ORs (joined) reported from Base Railhead loading H.T. 6.30 A.M. Transport for R.E Services 10 wagons for 252 Tunnelling Co. 2 " " 457 Field Co. | ASC |
|  | 24.9.17 |  |  | ASC |

H.H.W. Spence
LIEUT. COLONEL,
COMMDG. 62ND DIVISIONAL TRAIN.

Army Form C. 2118.

ORIGINAL (6)

# WAR DIARY
## or
## INTELLIGENCE SUMMARY.
(Erase heading not required.)

| Place | Date | Hour | Summary of Events and Information | Remarks and references to Appendices |
|---|---|---|---|---|
| BAPAUME | 25.9.17. | 6.30 A.M. | **82ND DIVISIONAL TRAIN.**<br>Railhead loading H.T. Transport for R.E services as under:-<br>10 wagons for 252 Tunnelling Co.<br>4 " " 457 Field Co.<br>8 H.D. horses drawn from 20th R.P. | H.T.L |
|  | 26.9.17 | 6.30 A.M. | Railhead loading H.T. Transport for R.E services as under.<br>4 wagons for 252 Tunnelling Co.<br>4 " " 457 Field Co. | H.T.L |
|  | 27.9.17 | 7.30 A.M. | Railhead loading H.T. Transport for R.E services as under.<br>1 Riding horse transferred to 2/6th Y.+L. Regt. | H.T.L |
|  | 28.9.17. | 7.30 A.M. | Railhead loading H.T. Transport for R.E. services as under:<br>4 wagons for 252 Tunnelling Co.<br>Convoy of 20 wagons proceeded to BUCQUOY to collect bread & eggs. | H.T.L |

J.H.Williams
LIEUT. COLONEL,
COMMDG. 82ND DIVISIONAL TRAIN.

Army Form C. 2118.

ORIGINAL (?)

# WAR DIARY
## or
## INTELLIGENCE SUMMARY
*(Erase heading not required.)*

## 62ND DIVISIONAL TRAIN.

| Place | Date | Hour | Summary of Events and Information | Remarks and references to Appendices |
|---|---|---|---|---|
| BAPAUME | 29.9.17. | 7.30 A.M. | Railhead loading H.T. Transport for R.E. services as under:— 4 wagons for 252 Tunnelling Co. 4 " " 461 Field Co. Inspection of 521, 527, & 528 Companies by D.D.S.T. 3rd Army. | AAK |
| | 30.9.17 | 7.30 A.M. | Railhead loading H.T. Transport for R.E. services as on 29.9.17. Convoy of 20 wagons proceeded to BUCQUOY for local hay | AAK |

A.W. Killen
LIEUT COLONEL.
COMMDG. 62ND DIVISIONAL TRAIN.

ORIGINAL.    CONFIDENTIAL.

Vol 10

WAR DIARY

OF

62ND DIVISIONAL TRAIN

FROM :- 1ST OCTOBER 1917.

TO :- 31ST OCTOBER 1917.

VOLUME No. 10.

[signature]
LIEUT. COLONEL.
COMMDG. 62ND DIVISIONAL TRAIN

# WAR DIARY or INTELLIGENCE SUMMARY

Army Form C. 2118.

ORIGINAL

| Place | Date | Hour | Summary of Events and Information | Remarks and references to Appendices |
|---|---|---|---|---|
| BAPAUME | 1/10/17 | | Routes: BAPAUME. Refilling Point — Divisional Troops Group. BAPAUME-BEUGNATRE road. 185, 186, 187 Brigade Groups. BAPAUME-FAVREUIL road. Supplies drawn from Railhead by H.T. 7.30 A.M. Transport for R.E. services as under :— 4 wagons for 252 Tunnelling Coy. 4 — 461 Field Company 4 — | M.M. |
| | 2/10/17 | | Railhead loading H.T. 7.30 A.M. Transport for R.E. services as on 1st. 2/5th V.V.L. reported for a few administration. 1 coy. (C.T.) Detached from 525 Coy. for one week to 63rd Divisional Depot Battalion. Convoy of 20 wagons detailed to collect local hay from BUCQUOY. | M.M. |
| | 3/10/17 | | Railhead loading H.T. 7.30 A.M. Transport for R.E. services as on 2nd. Convoy of 20 wagons detailed to collect local hay from ACHIET LE PETIT. Night detail to take 50 tanks fit of 2/6 W. R. Regt to MOREUIL & back to Depot. | M.M. |

M. Mulholland
LIEUT. COLONEL
COMMDG. 62nd DIVISIONAL TRAIN

Army Form C. 2118.

(2) ORIGINAL

# WAR DIARY
## or
## INTELLIGENCE SUMMARY.
*(Erase heading not required.)*

Instructions regarding War Diaries and Intelligence Summaries are contained in F. S. Regs., Part II. and the Staff Manual respectively. Title pages will be prepared in manuscript.

| Place | Date | Hour | Summary of Events and Information | Remarks and references to Appendices |
|---|---|---|---|---|
| BAPAUME E. | 4.10.17 | | Railhead loading H.T. 7-30 A.M. Transport for R.E. services as a 3rd | A.H.B. |
| | 5.10.17 | | Railhead loading H.T. 7.30 A.M. Transport for R.E. services 4 wagons for 461 Field Coy R.E. 20 wagons details to collect local hay from BUCQUOY. | A.H.B. |
| | 6.10.17 | | Railhead loading H.T. 7.30 A.M. Transport for R.E. services as a 5th. 5 wagons details to collect local hay for ACHIET-LE-PETIT. | A.H.B. |
| | 7.10.17 | | Railhead loading H.T. 7-30 A.M. Transport for R.E. services as a 6th. 20 wagons details to collect local hay from BUCQUOY. | A.H.B. |
| | 8.10.17 | | Railhead loading H.T. 7.30 A.M. Transport for R.E. services as a 7th. | A.H.B. |

A.H. Allen Smith
LIEUT. COLONEL
COMMDG. 62ND DIVISIONAL TRAIN.

A5834 Wt. W4973/M687 750,000 8/16 D. D. & L. Ltd. Forms/C.2118/13.

Army Form C. 2118.

(3)

ORIGINAL

# WAR DIARY
## or
## INTELLIGENCE SUMMARY.
(Erase heading not required.)

Instructions regarding War Diaries and Intelligence Summaries are contained in F. S. Regs., Part II. and the Staff Manual respectively. Title pages will be prepared in manuscript.

| Place | Date | Hour | Summary of Events and Information | Remarks and references to Appendices |
|---|---|---|---|---|
| BAPAUME | 9.10.17 | | Railheads loading 7.30 A.M. 187th Brigade Group by M.T. remainder by H.T. 578 Company A.S.C. moved to O.34.A. ROEUVIGNY. Sheet 57c 1/40000. 2 reinforcements arrived from Base. 1 Surplus Sergeant left to report to O.C. A.S.C. Base Depot HAVRE. | APP. |
| | 10.10.17 | | Refilling Point for 169th Brigade Group at O.34.A. remainder unchanged. Railheads loading as on 9th. 10 Drivers detailed to collect lorry from BUCQUOY. | APP. |
| | 11.10.17 | | Refilling Points as on 10th. Railhead loading 7.30 A.M. 185th & 187th Brigade Groups by M.T. remainder by H.T. 526 Company A.S.C. moved to O.28.C. Sheet 57c 1/40000. | APP. |
| | 12.10.17 | | Refilling Points for 185th Brigade Group O.28.C. remainder unchanged. Railhead loading 7.30 A.M. 185th 186th & 187th Brigade Groups by M.T., Div'l Troops Group by H.T. H.Qrs Div'l Train moved to O.28 A.6.5. Sheet 57c 1/40000. 527 Company A.S.C. moved to N.4.d.8.5. Sheet 57c 1/40000. | APP. |

J.H. Killingford
LIEUT. COLONEL,
COMMDG. 62ND DIVISIONAL TRAIN.

Army Form C. 2118.

ORIGINAL

# WAR DIARY
## or
## INTELLIGENCE SUMMARY.
(Erase heading not required.)

Instructions regarding War Diaries and Intelligence Summaries are contained in F. S. Regs., Part II. and the Staff Manual respectively. Title pages will be prepared in manuscript.

| Place | Date | Hour | Summary of Events and Information | Remarks and references to Appendices |
|---|---|---|---|---|
| ROCQUIGNY | 13.10.17 | | Railhead loading 7.30 A.M. 185th & 187th Brigade Groups by M.T. Brigade Groups by H.T. Refilling Point for 186th Brigade Group N 18 a.3.3 remainder unchanged | APR. |
| | 14.10.17 | | Railhead loading as on 13th. 2 reinforcements reported from Base. | APR. |
| | 15.10.17 | | Railhead leaving 8.0 A.M. Transport as on 14th. 17 wagons detailed to draw coal for ROCQUIGNY. Medical inspection & classification of all N.C.O's & men in S25, S26 & S27 companies | APR. |
| | 16.10.17 | | Railhead loading 7.30 A.M. Transport as on 15th. 25 wagons detailed to draw coal for ROCQUIGNY. Medical inspection & classification of all N.C.O's & men in Train H.qrs. & S28 company | APR. |
| | 17.10.17 | | Railhead loading 6.30 A.M. Transport as on 16th. | APR. |
| | 18.10.17 | | Railhead leaving 8 A.M. Transport as on 17th. 9 Reinforcements reported from Base | APR. |

H.P.Willingsmer
LIEUT. COLONEL,
COMMDG. 62ND DIVISIONAL TRAIN.

Army Form C. 2118.

ORIGINAL

# WAR DIARY
## or
## INTELLIGENCE SUMMARY.
(Erase heading not required.)

| Place | Date | Hour | Summary of Events and Information | Remarks and references to Appendices |
|---|---|---|---|---|
| ROCQUIGNY. | 19.10.17 | | Railhead loading as on 18th. | Aff. |
| | 20.10.17 | | Railhead loading as on 19th. | Aff. |
| | 21.10.17 | | Railhead loading as on 20th. | Aff. |
| | 22.10.17 | | Railhead loading as on 21st. | Aff. |
| | 23.10.17 | | Railhead loading as on 22nd. | Aff. |
| | 24.10.17 | | Railhead loading as on 23rd. 9 wagons detailed to bring coal for ROCQUIGNY. | Aff. |
| | 25.10.17 | | Railhead loading as on 24th. Rations for 312th Brigade R.F.A. delivered by 4 lorries to BOISLEUX-AU-MONT. | Aff. |
| | 26.10.17 | | Railhead loading as on 25th and rations delivered to 312th Brigade R.F.A. as on 25th. | Aff. |
| | 27.10.17 | | Railhead loading + rations delivered to 311th Brigade R.F.A. as on 26th. 525 Company A.S.C. moved to S.9.c.5.4. Sheet 51 B. | Aff. |
| | 28.10.17 | | Railhead loading 8 A.M. Divisional Troops 185th & 187th Brigade Groups by Motor Lorries 186th Brigade Group by 7th Divisional Troops Coy. moved to S.9.e.5.4. Sheet 51 B. Railway Point 526 Company A.S.C. marched to GOMIECOURT. | Aff. |

A.M.Mullins
LIEUT. COLONEL,
COMMDG. 62ND DIVISIONAL TRAIN.

Army Form C. 2118.

ORIGINAL

# WAR DIARY
## or
## INTELLIGENCE SUMMARY.
(Erase heading not required.)

Instructions regarding War Diaries and Intelligence Summaries are contained in F.S. Regs., Part II. and the Staff Manual respectively. Title pages will be prepared in manuscript.

| Place | Date | Hour | Summary of Events and Information | Remarks and references to Appendices |
|---|---|---|---|---|
| ROCQUIGNY. | 29.10.17. | ? | Railhead for Divisional Troops Group ARRAS. Supplies drawn by H.T. Railheads for remainder unchanged – M.T. for 185th & 187th Brigade Groups – H.T. for 186th Brigade Group. Refilling Point for 185th Brigade Group. ACHIET-LE-GRAND – GOMIECOURT road – remainder unchanged. 526 Company A.S.C. marched from GOMIECOURT to BARLY. 528 Company A.S.C. marched from RUCQUIGNY to GOMIECOURT. | JMcAF |
| | 30.10.17. | | Railhead for Divisional Troops Group BOISLEUX-AU-MONT. Supplies drawn by H.T. refilling point unchanged. Railhead for remainder unchanged. Supplies drawn by M.T. for all 3 Groups. Refilling Point for 185th Brigade BARLY. do for 187th Brigade ACHIET-LE-GRAND – GOMIECOURT road. do for 186th Brigade unchanged. Train Hqrs. marches from ROCQUIGNY to MONCHIET. 528 Company marches from GOMIECOURT to BERNEVILLE. 527 Company marches from BEAULENCOURT to GOMIECOURT. | JMcAF |

JMcAFie
LIEUT. COLONEL.
COMMDG. 62ND DIVISIONAL TRAIN.

# WAR DIARY
## or
## INTELLIGENCE SUMMARY.
*(Erase heading not required.)*

Army Form C. 2118.

| Place | Date | Hour | Summary of Events and Information | Remarks and references to Appendices |
|---|---|---|---|---|
| Rocquigny | 29.10.17 | | Railhead for Div. Troops, ARRAS | |
| | | | Refilling point 135 Rile. Robed & Grand-Gonicourt Rd. 326 Cy marched from | |
| | | | Gonicourt to Italy. 528 Cy marched from Rocquigny to Gonicourt. | |
| | 30.10.17 | | Railhead for Div Troops BOISLEUX AU MONT. Refilling points 175 Odd BARLY. | |
| | | | 187 Bde Robed & Grand-Bruay Rd. Leau H.Q. marched for Rocquigny 527 moved | |
| | | | 528 Cy moved from Gonicourt to Bermicourt. 326 Cy marched from Beaumeznil to Gonicourt | |
| Montchâl | 31.10.17 | | Railhead for Divisional Troops & the Ruse. Refilling point 187 Bde. Robed & Grand | |
| | | | Gonicourt Rd. 527 Cy moved from Gonicourt to Goy en Artois | |
| | 1.11.17 | | 326 Cy arrived from Rocd to Bermicourt. 528 Cy moved for Boy. | |
| | 2.11.17 | | 525 Cy moved from Boisleux to Brig. left on Balance | |
| | 3.11.17 | | Railhead for R.A. Robed Refilling point Beaumeznil. Refilling point for | |
| | | | 1st Div Engineers Robhill, St Grand-Gonicourt Rd. Divl. Companies 526 Moved to | |
| | | | Bermicourt. 528 Cy Bermicourt & Gonicourt, 527 Cy Boy & Robel Brit. R.E.S. Robel & Croix Res | |
| | 4.11.17 | | H.Q. Leau moved for Montchâl to Rocquigny. 528 Cy moved from Bermicourt to Montchâl | |
| | | | 526 Cy moved from Gonicourt Rocquigny. 527 Cy for Combles to Rams 74 | |
| Rocquigny | 10.11.17 | | Railhead for Div. Troops Rocquigny. Refilling point Robed & Croix Rd Grand-Gonicourt | |

Army Form C. 2118.

ORIGINAL

# WAR DIARY
## or
## INTELLIGENCE SUMMARY.
(Erase heading not required.)

Instructions regarding War Diaries and Intelligence Summaries are contained in F. S. Regs., Part II. and the Staff Manual respectively. Title pages will be prepared in manuscript.

| Place | Date | Hour | Summary of Events and Information | Remarks and references to Appendices |
|---|---|---|---|---|
| MONCHIET. | 31.10.17 | | Railhead 1 Raff Refilling Point for Divisional Troops Group unchanged. Railhead for remainder BEAUMETZ-LES-RIVIERE. Supplies drawn by M.T. at 11 A.M. Refilling Point for 186th Brigade Group. ACHIET-LE-GRAND — GOMIECOURT road. Remainder unchanged. 307 Company A.S.C. marches from GOMIECOURT to GOUY-EN-ARTOIS. | H.M. |

A.H. Pullen Jones
LIEUT. COLONEL,
COMMDG. 62ND DIVISIONAL TRAIN

ORIGINAL   CONFIDENTIAL.   Vol 11

# WAR DIARY

OF

# 62ND DIVISIONAL TRAIN

From :- Nov. 1st 1917.

To :- Nov. 30th 1917.

Volume :- XI.

[signature]
LIEUT. COLONEL
COMMDG. 62ND DIVISIONAL TRAIN

# WAR DIARY or INTELLIGENCE SUMMARY

Army Form C. 2118.

**62ND DIVISIONAL TRAIN**

| Place | Date | Hour | Summary of Events and Information | Remarks and references to Appendices |
|---|---|---|---|---|
| MONCHIET | 1.11.17 | | Railhead for Infantry Brigade Groups - BEAUMETZ | |
| | | | do Divisional Artillery - BOISLEUX-AU-MONT | |
| | | | Refilling Points for 185th Brigade Group - BARLY | AAA |
| | | | 186th Brigade Group - GOUY | AAA |
| | | | 187th Brigade Group - BERNEVILLE | AAA |
| | | | Divisional Artillery - BOISLEUX-AU-MONT | AAA |
| | | | Railheads by H.T. | AAA |
| | | | Supplies drawn for Railheads | |
| | 2.11.17 | | Railhead loading H.T. 11 A.M. | |
| | | | Refilling Points unchanged | |
| | 3.11.17 | | do | |
| | 4.11.17 | | do | |
| | 5.11.17 | | do | |
| | 6.11.17 | | do | |

LIEUT. COLONEL
COMMDG. 62ND DIVISIONAL TRAIN

Army Form C. 2118.

(2)

ORIGINAL

# WAR DIARY
## or
## INTELLIGENCE SUMMARY.
(Erase heading not required)

62ND DIVISIONAL TRAIN.

Instructions regarding War Diaries and Intelligence Summaries are contained in F. S. Regs., Part II. and the Staff Manual respectively. Title pages will be prepared in manuscript.

| Place | Date | Hour | Summary of Events and Information | Remarks and references to Appendices |
|---|---|---|---|---|
| MONCHIET | 7.11.17 | | Railheads and Refilling Points unchanged. 526 Company moved from BARLY to BERNEVILLE. 528 Company moved from BERNEVILLE to BARLY. Refilling Points of 185th & 187th Brigades Groups unchanged. Other Units unchanged. | A.F.F.2 |
| | 8.11.17 | | No change | A.F.F.2 |
| | 9.11.17 | | do | A.F.F.2 |
| | 10.11.17 | | do | A.F.F.2 |
| | 11.11.17 | | 3 Reinforcements reported from Base. 23 "B" leaders reported for duty. 252 Employment Coy. 525 Coy A.S.C. moved from BOISIEUX to BARLY. St. GERTRUDE & "A" horses moved to New huts. | A.F.F.2 |

Signed,
LIEUT. COLONEL.
COMMDG. 62ND DIVISIONAL TRAIN.

A 5834 Wt. W4973/M687 750,000 8/16 D. D. & L. Ltd. Forms/C.2118/13.

Army Form C. 2118.
(3)

# WAR DIARY
## or
## INTELLIGENCE SUMMARY.
(Erase heading not required.)

### 62ND DIVISIONAL TRAIN.
Summary of Events and Information

ORIGINAL

| Place | Date | Hour | Summary of Events and Information | Remarks and references to Appendices |
|---|---|---|---|---|
| MONCHIET | 13.11.17 | | Reinforced for Divisional Artillery. ACHIET. Cleared by Lorries. Refilling Point – BEAULENCOURT. Reinforced for remainder unchanged. Refilling Points for Infantry Brigade Groups ACHIET-LE-GRAND – GOMIECOURT road. Moves of Companies as follows:— 525 Company BOIRY to BEAULENCOURT. 526 – REMEVILLE to GOMIECOURT. 527 – GUY to ACHIET-LE-PETIT. 528 – BARLY to COURCELLES. | A.H.H. |
| | 14.11.17 | | Reinforced for Divisional Artillery ROCQUIGNY Refilling Point BARASTRE. Reinforced for Infantry Brigade Groups ACHIET. All supplies drawn by Lorries. Refilling Point 185 & 187 Brigade Groups ROCQUIGNY. 186 Brigade Group – ACHIET-LE-GRAND – GOMIECOURT road. H.Q. Train marched from MONCHIET to ROCQUIGNY. | |

R.R.H... Gee
LIEUT. COLONEL,
COMMDG. 62ND DIVISIONAL TRAIN.

A5834 Wt. W4973/M687 750,000 8/16 D D. & L. Ltd. Forms/C.2118/13.

**Army Form C. 2118.**

(4)

# WAR DIARY
## or
## INTELLIGENCE SUMMARY.
(Erase heading not required.)  ORIGINAL

## 62ND DIVISIONAL TRAIN.

Instructions regarding War Diaries and Intelligence Summaries are contained in F.S. Regs., Part II. and the Staff Manual respectively. Title pages will be prepared in manuscript.

| Place | Date | Hour | Summary of Events and Information | Remarks and references to Appendices |
|---|---|---|---|---|
| MONCHIET | 14.11.17 | 6a.m. | 525 Company moves from BEAULENCOURT to BARASTRE. 526 from GOMIECOURT to ROCQUIGNY. 528 from COURCELLES to BARASTRE. | Appx 2 |
| ROCQUIGNY | 15.11.17 | | RAILHEAD ACHIET for Infantry Brigade Groups. ROCQUIGNY for Divisional Artillery. Refilling Points unchanged. | |
| | 16.11.17 | | Railhead ACHIET for Divisional Artillery and 185th & 187th Brigade Groups. ROCQUIGNY for 186th Brigade Group. Refilling Point of 186th Brigade Group. ROCQUIGNY - remainder unchanged. 517 Company moves from FICHEUX-LE-PETIT to LECHELLE. | Appx 3 |
| | 17.11.17 | | Railheads for whole Division - ROCQUIGNY. Refilling Points unchanged. Whole Train moves to BUS. | Appx 4 |

J.W. Killen Jones
LIEUT. COLONEL.
COMMDG. 62ND DIVISIONAL TRAIN.

Army Form C. 2118.

ORIGINAL (5)

# WAR DIARY
## or
## INTELLIGENCE SUMMARY.
(Erase heading not required)

**62ND DIVISIONAL TRAIN**

Summary of Events and Information

| Place | Date | Hour | Summary of Events and Information | Remarks and references to Appendices |
|---|---|---|---|---|
| BUS | 18.11.17 | | RAILHEAD – ROCQUIGNY. Refilling Point 6. Divisional Artillery BARASTRE. Ration R.H.s NEUVILLE. Rod-Heads: BERTINCOURT BERTINCOURT. 185th Brigade, 186th Brigade, 187th Brigade. 10 wagons detailed for 460 Field C. R.E. at 5 p.m. for work on roads. | AM |
| | 19.11.17 | | Refilling points as on 18th. Rations for consumption 20th & 21st delivered to units rail heads. 34 wagons reported to 457 Field Co. at 9 a.m. for work on roads to be employed for 48 hours. | AM |
| | 20.11.17 | | Railhead at FREMICOURT. Rations for whole Division dumped on Bus–BARASTRE road. Advance in Divisional front commenced 6.10 a.m. | AM |

A. Miller
LIEUT. COLONEL.
COMMDG. 62ND DIVISIONAL TRAIN.

Army Form C. 2118.

ORIGINAL

# WAR DIARY
## or
## INTELLIGENCE SUMMARY.
(Erase heading not required)
## 62ND DIVISIONAL TRAIN

| Place | Date | Hour | Summary of Events and Information | Remarks and references to Appendices |
|---|---|---|---|---|
| RUS | 21/11/17 | | Railhead unchanged. Refilling Points for Divisional Troops & 185th Brigade, Ratu Ros NEUVILLE.<br>" " 186th & 187th Brigades. NEUVILLE-RUYAULCOURT roads.<br>Supply Sections of Train moves forward to NEUVILLE. | A/F/L |
| | 22/11/17 | | Railhead & refilling points unchanged.<br>Division relieved at night. | A/F/L |
| | 23/11/17 | | Railhead unchanged.<br>Refilling Points Divisional Troops & 185th Brigade unchanged.<br>186th & 187th Brigades. BERTINCOURT.<br>525 Company moves to YTRESCAULT.<br>Supply Section of other Companies returned to RUS.<br>Lieut. F. Bartlett departs for HAVRE. | A/F/L |

J.H. Wilsea Pack
LIEUT. COLONEL.
COMMDG. 62ND DIVISIONAL TRAIN.

Army Form C. 2118.

# WAR DIARY
## or
## INTELLIGENCE SUMMARY.
*(Erase heading not required.)*

### 62ND DIVISIONAL pTRAIN.

ORIGINAL

Instructions regarding War Diaries and Intelligence Summaries are contained in F. S. Regs., Part II. and the Staff Manual respectively. Title pages will be prepared in manuscript.

| Place | Date | Hour | Summary of Events and Information | Remarks and references to Appendices |
|---|---|---|---|---|
| BUS | 24.11.17 | | Railhead unchanged. Refilling Points – Divisional Troops – TRESCAULT 185th Brigade. BUS – BARASTRE road 186th & 187th Brigades unchanged. | HFF |
| | | | 10 H.D movements drawn for ALBERT | HFF |
| | 25.11.17 | | Railhead & refilling points unchanged. Sixth section of Brigade Companies carried forward to METZ-TRESCAULT road Divisional moved forward into line | HFF |
| | 26.11.17 | | Railhead unchanged. Refilling Points for 185th, 186th, 187th Brigade Corps Q.21.a & 6. Sheet 57. Divisional Troops unchanged | HFF |
| | 27.11.17 | | Railhead & Refilling Points unchanged. | HFF |
| | 28.11.17 | | Railhead & Refilling Points for Divisional Troops & 188th Brigade unchanged for 186th & 187th Brigade BUS-BARASTRE road. Sixth section of H 526 & 528 Companies returned to BUS. | HFF |

H.F. Wilberforce
LIEUT. COLONEL.
COMMDG. 62ND DIVISIONAL TRAIN.

Army Form C. 2118.

(8)

ORIGINAL

# WAR DIARY
## or
## INTELLIGENCE SUMMARY.
(Erase heading not required)
### 62ND DIVISIONAL TRAIN
Summary of Events and Information

Instructions regarding War Diaries and Intelligence Summaries are contained in F. S. Regs, Part II. and the Staff Manual respectively. Title pages will be prepared in manuscript.

| Place | Date | Hour | Summary of Events and Information | Remarks and references to Appendices |
|---|---|---|---|---|
| BUS | 29.11.17 | | RAILHEAD - BAPAUME. Refilling Points - Divisional Troops unchanged. 185th + 187th Brigades BERTINCOURT 186th Brigade BUS - BARASTRE and Supply Section of 5th Company returned to BUS. | AppN. |
| | 30.11.17 | | Railhead & Refilling Points unchanged. Owing to heavy shell fire 575 Company moved to NEUVILLE - METZ (nom) and suffered more damage in same area). | AppO. |

A. H. Kellaway
LIEUT. COLONEL,
COMMDG. 62ND DIVISIONAL TRAIN.

CONFIDENTIAL.

YM 12

WAR DIARY
OF
62ND DIVISIONAL TRAIN.

From:- 1-12-17.
To :- 31-12-17.

Volume:- 12.

ORIGINAL.

# WAR DIARY or INTELLIGENCE SUMMARY

62nd DIVISIONAL TRAIN.

Army Form C. 2118.

| Place | Date | Hour | Summary of Events and Information | Remarks and references to Appendices |
|---|---|---|---|---|
| BUS | 1/12/17 | | Rulens BAPAUME. Refilling Points. Divisional Troops Group. NEUVILLE. 185th & 187th Brigade Groups. BERTINCOURT. 186th Brigade Group. BUS. BARASTRE road | APX/4 |
| | 2/12/17 | | Refilling Points for 3 Brigade Groups on BERTINCOURT – VELU road. Divisional Troops Group unchanged. | APX/5 |
| | 3/12/17 | | Refilling Points unchanged. Supplies drawn from BAPAUME and dumps for 3 Brigade Groups on AVETTE – MOYENNEVILLE road. Supply sections of 526, 527 & 528 Companies marched to COURCELLES & bivouacked for the night. STURTON reported Jnr Rank. & Division moved to XVII Corps area. Divisional Artillery & 525 Company A.S.C. attached to V Corps. | APX/6 |
| | 4/12/17 | | Moves as follows:- Train Headquarters to MONCHIET. 526 Company to ARRAS. 527 Company to BAILLEULVAL. 528 Company to BLAIREVILLE. | APX/7 |

Army Form C. 2118.

# WAR DIARY
## or
## INTELLIGENCE SUMMARY.
(Erase heading not required.)

### 62ND DIVISIONAL TRAIN.

| Place | Date | Hour | Summary of Events and Information | Remarks and references to Appendices |
|---|---|---|---|---|
| MONCHIET | 5/7/17 | | Railhead BEAUMETZ-LEZ-LOGES<br>Refilling Points. 185th Brigade Group - ARRAS.<br>186th - BAILLEULMONT.<br>187th - BLAIREVILLE.<br>Moves as follows:- 527 Company to MONTENESCOURT.<br>528 Company to DUISANS. | Appx |
| | 6/7/17 | | Division moved to XIII Corps area.<br>Refilling Points. 185th Brigade Group unchanged<br>186th Brigade Group TINCQUES - CHELERS road<br>187th Brigade Group HERMIN<br>Moves as follows:-<br>Train Headquarters to SAVY.<br>526 Company to SAVY.<br>527 Company to TINCQUETTE<br>528 Company to HERMIN | Appx |

J.J.Killen Jones
LIEUT. COLONEL
COMMDG. 62ND DIVISIONAL TRAIN

Army Form C. 2118.

# WAR DIARY
## or
## INTELLIGENCE SUMMARY.
(Erase heading not required.)

### 62ND DIVISIONAL TRAIN.

| Place | Date | Hour | Summary of Events and Information | Remarks and references to Appendices |
|---|---|---|---|---|
| SAVY. | 7/12/17 | | Railhead MONT ST ELOI. Refilling Points 188th Brigade Group AUBIGNY - MINGOVAL road. Remainder unchanged. | Appx. Appx. |
| | 8/12/17 | | No change | |
| | 9/12/17 | | Refilling Point for 187th Brigade Group. HESDIGNEUL. Remainder unchanged. 525 Company moved to HESDIGNEUL. Capt. D.N. Roberts commanding 527 Company proceeded to England to report at Infantry Training School Bexgris. Lieut. A. Ogan assumed command of 527 Company. | Appx. |
| | 10/12/17 | | Refilling Point for 186th Brigade Group - ANNEZIN. Remainder unchanged. 527 Company moved to ANNEZIN. | Appx. |
| | 11/12/17 | | Railheads for 186th & 187th Brigade Groups. LILLERS. 185th Brigade Group unchanged. Refilling Points unchanged. | Appx. |

N.D. Clayton Wyler
LIEUT. COLONEL
COMMANDG. 62ND DIVISIONAL TRAIN.

A.S834  Wt. W4973/M687  750,000  8/16  D. D. & L. Ltd.  Forms/C.2118/4

Army Form C. 2118.

# WAR DIARY
## ~~INTELLIGENCE SUMMARY~~
(Erase heading not required.)

### 62ND DIVISIONAL TRAIN

| Place | Date | Hour | Summary of Events and Information | Remarks and references to Appendices |
|---|---|---|---|---|
| SAVY | 12/1/17 | | Railhead & Refilling Points unchanged. Train Headquarters moved to ST. SAUVEUR. | AFB |
| ST SAUVEUR | 13/1/17 | | No change. Capt. T.T.J. Sheffield proceeded to Headquarters Tank Corps for interview | AFB |
| | 14/1/17 | | Railhead for 3 Brigade Groups - ALLERS. Refilling Points 185th Brigade Group ANNEZIN. 186th " " BUSNETTES. 187th " " - (unchanged) | AFB |
| | 15/1/17 | | 526 Company moved to ANNEZIN. 527 Company moved to L'ECLEME. Railhead & refilling points unchanged. 527 Company moved to BUSNES. | AFB |
| | 16/1/17 | | Railhead & refilling Points unchanged. Train Headquarters moved to BAS RIEUX. | AFB |

M.R. Rutherford
LIEUT. COLONEL
COMMDG. 62ND DIVISIONAL TRAIN

Army Form C. 2118.

# WAR DIARY
## or
## INTELLIGENCE SUMMARY.

62ND ~~Divl. Sect.~~ N Ad. ~~chn~~ TRAIN.

Original

| Place | Date | Hour | Summary of Events and Information | Remarks and references to Appendices |
|---|---|---|---|---|
| BAS RIEUX | 7/12/17 | | No change. | App 3 |
| | 10/12/17 | | Railhead & Refilling Points unchanged. 526 Company moved to RECOURT 527 - ANNEZIN 528 - HERMIN. Severe frost. | App 6 |
| | 14/12/17 | | Railhead for 3 Brigade Groups MONT ST ELOI Refilling Points 185th Brigade Group RECOURT - MONCHY BRETON road 186th - TINQUES - CHELERS road 187th - HERMIN Train Headquarters moved to SAVY. 527 Company moved to TINQUETTE. | App 8 |
| SAVY | 20/12/17 | | No change. Lieut. Stephen reported for base. | App 10 |

A.H. Phillips-Jones
Lieut Col
Divisional Train

**Army Form C. 2118.**

# WAR DIARY
# or
# INTELLIGENCE SUMMARY.
(Erase heading not required.)

## 62ND DIVISIONAL TRAIN.

Summary of Events and Information

Instructions regarding War Diaries and Intelligence Summaries are contained in F. S. Regs., Part II. and the Staff Manual respectively. Title pages will be prepared in manuscript.

| Place | Date | Hour | Summary of Events and Information | Remarks and references to Appendices |
|---|---|---|---|---|
| SAVY | 21/1/17 | | No change. | A.P.S. |
| | 22/1/17 | | Rations for 3 Brigade Groups TINCQUES. Refilling Points made good. Supplies drawn from Railhead for 186th Brigade Group by H.T. Supplies drawn from Refilling Points by 1st line Transport | A.P.S. |
| | 23/1/17 | | No change | A.P.S. |
| | 24/1/17 | | Supplies for 3 Brigade Groups drawn from Railhead by H.T. Thaw commenced | A.P.S. |
| | 25/1/17 | | Thaw continued. | |
| | 26/1/17 | | Has stopped slumped. Commanding officer proceeded on line refitting Assumed command | A.P.S. |
| | 27/1/17 | | No change | A.P.S. |
| | 28/1/17 | | do 52s Coy (M.T.) train moved to Gouzeaucourt to Con 6. Next troops incl. 625 Coy Ruthless at MARAS. 52s Coy moved to FOSSEUX | A.P.S. |
| | 29/1/17 | | do | A.P.S. |

Lt R. G. BRUCE returned from duty from 4th R. P.
for COMMDG. 62ND DIVISIONAL TRAIN

Army Form C. 2118.

# WAR DIARY
## or
## INTELLIGENCE SUMMARY.
*(Erase heading not required.)*

## 62ND DIVISIONAL TRAIN.

Original

Instructions regarding War Diaries and Intelligence Summaries are contained in F.S. Regs., Part II. and the Staff Manual respectively. Title pages will be prepared in manuscript.

| Place | Date | Hour | Summary of Events and Information | Remarks and references to Appendices |
|---|---|---|---|---|
| SAVY | 30/11/17 | | 52st C moved from FOSSEUX to SAVY. 2nd RA moved into area south RA on 2nd Pack at TINCQUES. Rpt for 2nd Corps established at SAVY. 1 Reinforcement reported from BASE. No change 3 Inf Bdes. | 1 ltr |
| | 31/11/17 | | No change. 6 Reinforcements reported from BASE | 1 ltr |

J.B. Clayton Major
for.
LIEUT. COLONEL,
COMMDG. 62ND DIVISIONAL TRAIN.

Army Form C. 2118.

# WAR DIARY
## or
## INTELLIGENCE SUMMARY.
*(Erase heading not required.)*

Instructions regarding War Diaries and Intelligence Summaries are contained in F.S. Regs., Part II. and the Staff Manual respectively. Title pages will be prepared in manuscript.

| Place | Date | Hour | Summary of Events and Information | Remarks and references to Appendices |
|---|---|---|---|---|
| Bapaume | 1.7.17 | | Railhead closing N.I. 7am. | |
| " | 6.7.17 | | Remarks collected for Defence without 10am. Changes 12 noon, of R.O. 3 PM. | |
| " | 10.7.17 | | Railhead Lowrie N.I. 11am. | |
| " | 20.7.17 | | Inspected 1st line transport of the 102 R Regt Kole | |
| " | 23.7.17 | | Inspection of all of all Coys of the Town by Divisional Commandant | |
| " | 31.7.17 | | 2/L. Bradley proceeded to England to report as Officer & Training School, Bradford | |
| " | | | Corps Commander's inspection | |
| " | 2.8.17 | | 2/Lt. Young reported from Havre | |
| " | 6.8.17 | | P.S. 9 R. moore reported to take the of Lewis gunner. 3 weeks duty school | |
| " | 7.8.17 | | 2/Lt R. Morehouse + 2/Lt Bolton left 25 Coy Reinft to R.L.C. | |
| " | 10.8.17 | | 2/Lt R.M. Hatton & 2/Lt Taylor reported for duty | |
| " | 13.8.17 | | 2/Lt E.A. Burris reported from Havre | |
| " | 22.8.17 | | Capt. Geo. Bison Coll to join the 7th Division | |
| " | 30.8.17 | | 2/Lt. R.V. Pyke reported from Havre | |
| " | 6.9.17 | | 2/Lt. G. Iroh proceeded to England to Learning School, Bedford | |
| " | 10.9.17 | | 2/Lt Gray & Clarke reported from Havre | |

Army Form C. 2118.

# WAR DIARY
or
## INTELLIGENCE SUMMARY.
(Erase heading not required.)

Instructions regarding War Diaries and Intelligence Summaries are contained in F. S. Regs., Part II. and the Staff Manual respectively. Title pages will be prepared in manuscript.

| Place | Date | Hour | Summary of Events and Information | Remarks and references to Appendices |
|---|---|---|---|---|
| Bpaume. | 14.9.17 | | 2/Lieuts Horsburg & Ross proceeded to H.Q. R.F.C. | |
| | 16.9.17 | | B. Hodgson proceeded S.H.Q. R.F.C. (S.) Lt. on admission | |
| | 17.9.17 | | U. Category A. clerks sent to Base | |
| | 20.9.17 | | 2/Lt. C. Brain reported for duty | |
| | 24.9.17 | | Inspection of 527, 527 + 528 Coys by D.D.G.S. 3rd Army | |
| | 2.10.17 | | 2/Lt. Spoon (527 y.R.) reported for a fortnight's instruction | |
| | 9.10.17 | | 527 Coy moved to O.34.A Rocquigny | |
| | 10.10.17 | | Refilling point 527 BHQ. O.34.A | |
| | 11.10.17 | | 526 Coy moved to O.28.c. | |
| | 12.10.17 | | Refilling point 526 BHQ. O.28.c. | |
| | | | H.Q. Div. Train moved to O.28. A.6.5. (Sh.57cJ) | |
| | | | 527 Coy A.S.C. moved to M.4.A.D.D. (Sheet 67C.) | |
| Rocquigny | 13.10.17 | | Refilling point for 118 B. Div. N.13.a.3.3. | |
| " | 27.10.17 | | 526 Coy moved to L.9.C.5.4. Sheet 57.B | |
| " | 28.10.17 | | Refilling point for 18th Div. Corps moved to L.9. C Sunk | |
| " | | | 526 Coy marched to Gomiecourt. | |

Army Form C. 2118.

# WAR DIARY
## or
## INTELLIGENCE SUMMARY.
(Erase heading not required.)

Instructions regarding War Diaries and Intelligence Summaries are contained in F. S. Regs., Part II. and the Staff Manual respectively. Title pages will be prepared in manuscript.

| Place | Date | Hour | Summary of Events and Information | Remarks and references to Appendices |
|---|---|---|---|---|
| Rocquigny | 16.11.17 | | 327 Coy away from Rahel. 6. Rest. to Rockett | |
| | 17.11.17 | | Railhead for USAV Divison. Rocquigny. all Coys. report to same. | |
| | 20.11.17 | | Railhead Francart. Arrived on Ew. front commenced 6.20 am | |
| | 21.11.17 | | Suppy section of Train went to Neuville | |
| | 23.11.17 | | 325 Cy moved to Ingecourt. supply column of USa Cys returned to Rocq. 2/Lt R.H.G.M. reported for duty | |
| | 24.11.17 | | Railhead Bapaume | |
| | 28.11.17 | | 325 Coy moved to Neuville. Mil. Rd. Coy. 6 Coy 6 hrs. to life + hot fire | |
| | 3.12.17 | | Whole Division reprisa for Corps | |
| | 4.12.17 | | Moved J.H.Q. to Marchet. 326 Coy to Arras. 327 Cy to Bullecourt. 527 Cy to Ricourts | |
| Marchet | 5.12.17 | | Railhead Beaurell. by Coys. 327 Coy moved to Mantrescarl. 325 Cy to Sarsines | |
| | 6.12.17 | | 2000 J.H.Q. to Sang. 326 Cy to Sang. 327 Cy to Ingecourt. 325 Cy to Itzouin | |
| Sang | 7.12.17 | | Railhead Mot. St. Eln. | |
| | 9.12.17 | | 325 Coy moved to Acheigueal. Capt. Ribe to proceed to Belford | |
| | 10.12.17 | | 327 Coy moved to Arneyen | |
| | 12.12.17 | | J.H.Q. moved to A. Sauveaut. | |
| A. Sauveaut | 13.12.17 | | Capt. Sheffard proceeded to S.t. Cypro. | |

T.7131. W. W768—776. 500000. 4/15. Sir J.C.&9.

**Army Form C. 2118.**

1917

# WAR DIARY
or
## INTELLIGENCE SUMMARY.
(Erase heading not required.)

Instructions regarding War Diaries and Intelligence Summaries are contained in F. S. Regs., Part II. and the Staff Manual respectively. Title pages will be prepared in manuscript.

| Place | Date | Hour | Summary of Events and Information | Remarks and references to Appendices |
|---|---|---|---|---|
| St Sauveur | 12.12.17 | | Railhead St Sauveur. 526 Coy. moved to Sauveur. 527 Coy. to St Fuscien | |
| | 13.12.17 | | 527 Coy. moved to Rumaux | |
| | 16.12.17 | | I.H.Q. moved to Boo River | |
| Boo River | 17.12.17 | | 526 Coy. moved to Rizeul. 527 Coy. move to Aumelyn. 528 Coy. move to Hornoy | |
| | 14.12.17 | | Railhead Moil H. Clin. I.H.Q. moved to Liercy. 527 Coy. moved to Incoquette | |
| | 20.12.17 | | 2/Lt. Stephew reported for duty | |
| Liercy | 22.2.17 | | Railhead Incogue | |
| | 27.12.17 | | 526 Coy. moved to Cavillers a Conte. | |
| | 28.12.17 | | 525 Coy. moved to Govenck. 2/Lt. Brown reported from wh. R.P. | |
| | 30.12.17 | | 525 Coy. moved to Liercy | |

ORIGINAL

CONFIDENTIAL.

Vol 13

# War Diary

## of

## 62nd Divisional Train.

From :- Jany 1st 1918.
To :- Jany 31st 1918.

Volume: 13.

Colonel
COMMDG. 62nd DIVISIONAL TRAIN.

Army Form C. 2118.

ORIGINAL

# WAR DIARY
## INTELLIGENCE SUMMARY.
*(Erase heading not required.)*

### 62ND DIVISIONAL TRAIN
Summary of Events and Information

| Place | Date | Hour | Summary of Events and Information | Remarks and references to Appendices |
|---|---|---|---|---|
| SAVY | 1-11-18 | | Railhead TINCOURT — RPs Fut Supp SAVY 165 RCE " ROISORT 286 " CHELERS 207 " HERMIN | |
| | 2-11-18 | | No change in Railhead refill. | |
| | 3-11-18 | | Do 2 reinforcements arrived from Base | |
| | 4-11-18 | | Do | |
| | 5-11-18 | | No change. Railhead refill. Fut Supp 185 & 286 "Coy". 187 Fd dumps moved to advanced area & erected at Boisjean-sur-Bourg. 326 by F.L. moved from Belloy to HERMIN to crush (hub) & always on return. Railhead for 187 Field finds drawn by F.L. Dumped here at EURIE. | |
| | 6-11-18 | | No change. | |
| | 7-11-18 | | No change. Railhead refill. Fut Supp 165 & 286 187 Rfe gun " 185 " dumps moved to Advanced area. 326 by F.L. & a new "hub" established to Coys (hub) at Blokeson Coys & Report to Coys (Hub) at Blokeson Coys (& Comp time) after off 5th Fut and at EURIE. A.W. Clayton Major | |

Army Form C. 2118.

ORIGINAL

# WAR DIARY
## or
## INTELLIGENCE SUMMARY.
(Erase heading not required.)

Instructions regarding War Diaries and Intelligence Summaries are contained in F. S. Regs., Part II. and the Staff Manual respectively. Title pages will be prepared in manuscript.

## 62nd DIVISIONAL TRAIN.

| Place | Date | Hour | Summary of Events and Information | Remarks and references to Appendices |
|---|---|---|---|---|
| SAVY | 8.1.18 | | No change | |
| Madagascar | 9.1.18 | | Train HQ moved from billets at SAVY to billets at Madagascar. No change in supply arrangements during the day. Supply Railhead remained at TINCOURT during the day. 57th Fd Amb at TINCOURES. 162nd Fd Amb moved from CHELERS to MADAGASCAR line. 521 Coy R.E. moved from billets at TINQUETTE to huts Rockdale Madagascar Corner. Railheads for Fd Amb sick changed from TINCOURES to EQUAIE. | |
| | 10.1.18 | | No change | |
| | 11.1.18 | | No Railhead supply. Class Instruction commenced. Commanding Officer returned. | |
| | | | for J.H. Clayton Lt.Col. | |
| | | | LIEUT. COLONEL. COMMDG. 62nd DIVISIONAL TRAIN. | |
| | 12.1.18 | | 3 Divn Reinforcements reported from Base. 8 G.S. Wagons details at 3 h to take infantry of the line for Rockefels Cook returning 10th a.m. 5 G.S. Wagons details for R.E. Services. | |

H.H. Williamson
LIEUT. COLONEL.
COMMDG. 62nd DIVISIONAL TRAIN.

**Army Form C. 2118.**

(3)

ORIGINAL

# WAR DIARY
## or
## INTELLIGENCE SUMMARY.
*(Erase heading not required.)*

Instructions regarding War Diaries and Intelligence Summaries are contained in F.S. Regs., Part II. and the Staff Manual respectively. Title pages will be prepared in manuscript.

## 62ND DIVISIONAL TRAIN.

| Place | Date | Hour | Summary of Events and Information | Remarks and references to Appendices |
|---|---|---|---|---|
| MADAGASCAR | 13.1.18 | | 2 G.S. Wagons detailed to report at ROCLINCOURT Dump at 3p.m. for R.E. services | Apps |
| | | 8 | do. to take infantry up the line from Rickfields Camp returning at 10 p.m. | Apps |
| | 14.1.18 | | Normal traffic resumed for midday. | Apps |
| | | | 2 Wagons detailed for R.E. services | Apps |
| | 15.1.18 | | 525 Company and Divisional troops Refilling Point moved to GREENWICH CAMP MADAGASCAR | Apps |
| | | | 4 Wagons detailed for R.E. services | |
| | | 8 | Wagons detailed to take infantry up the line from WAKEFIELD CAMP returning at 10 p.m. | |
| | | | Three Fruacation ordered for 6. A.M. | |
| | 16.1.18 | | 4 Wagons detailed for R.E. services | Apps |
| | 17.1.18 | | 2/Lieut GOODYEAR reported from Base for R.E. services | Apps |
| | | | 2 Wagons detailed for R.E. services | Apps |
| | 18.1.18 | | 4 Wagons detailed for R.E. services | Apps |
| | | | 1 P.B. reinforcement reported from Base. | Apps |

H.H. Killinger
LIEUT. COLONEL
COMMDG. 62ND DIVISIONAL TRAIN.

Army Form C. 2118.

ORIGINAL

# WAR DIARY
## or
## INTELLIGENCE SUMMARY

(Erase heading not required.)

Summary of Events and Information

## 62ND DIVISIONAL TRAIN.

| Place | Date | Hour | Summary of Events and Information | Remarks and references to Appendices |
|---|---|---|---|---|
| MADAGASCAR | 19.1.18. | | 2 Rogers detailed for R.E. Services. | AAA |
| | 20.1.18 | | 2 Rogers detailed for R.E. Services | AAA |
| | | | 3 PR reinforcements reported from Base | |
| | 21.1.18 | | 6 Rogers detailed for R.E. Services. | AAA |
| | 22.1.18 | | 4 Rogers detailed to take infantry up the line for HAREFIELD CAMP | AAA |
| | | | Transport as on 22nd January | AAA |
| | 23.1.18 | | | |
| | 24.1.18. | | Normal shuffer resumed from 6 A.M. | AAA |
| | | | 2 Rogers detailed for R.E. Services | |
| | | | 3 Rogers for 149 Labour Company | |
| | | | 6 Rogers for 361 Road Construction Company | |
| | | | 2/Lieut BRUCE evacuated hospital | |
| | 25.1.18 | | Transport as on 24th January | AAA |
| | 26.1.18 | | Divisional Commander inspected Refilling Points and Camps of wagon lines of Trains | AAA |
| | | | Transport as on 25th January | |

A5834  Wt W4973 M687 750,000 8/16  D. D. & L. Ltd.  Forms/C2118/13.

A.W. Mullinfors
LIEUT. COLONEL
COMMDG. 62ND DIVISIONAL TRAIN.

Army Form C. 2118.

ORIGINAL

# WAR DIARY
or
INTELLIGENCE SUMMARY.
(Erase heading not required.)

Summary of Events and Information
62ND DIVISIONAL TRAIN.

| Place | Date | Hour | Summary of Events and Information | Remarks and references to Appendices |
|---|---|---|---|---|
| MADAGASCAR | 27.1.18 | | Transport details as under :- <br> 2 wagons for R.E. Services <br> 4 wagons for 31st Division G <br> 6 wagons for 341 Road Construction Company | AAG |
| | 28.1.18 | | Transport details as on 26th January | AAG |
| | 29.1.18 | | 8 wagons detailed to deliver stuff to Divisional H.Q. <br> 2 wagons for R.E. Services | AAG |
| | 30.1.18 | | Transport details as under :- <br> 2 wagons for R.E. Services <br> 6 wagons for 341 Road Construction Company <br> 4 Reinforcements (2 Drivers I.C.QMS + 1 Lkh S.S) reported from Base. | AAG |
| | 31.1.18 | | Transport details as on 30th January <br> Capt. E.D.V. BATESON proceeded to ASC Base Depot for Medical Board | AAG |

F.H. Mullen Jones
LIEUT. COLONEL,
COMMDG. 62ND DIVISIONAL TRAIN.

CONFIDENTIAL

Vol 14

WAR DIARY

OF

THE 62nd DIVISIONAL TRAIN

FROM

FEBRUARY 1st to FEBRUARY 28th 1918.

VOLUME

14

ORIGINAL

3.3.18.

LIEUT. COLONEL,
COMMDG. 62nd DIVISIONAL TRAIN.

Army Form C. 2118.

# WAR DIARY
## or
## INTELLIGENCE SUMMARY.
(Erase heading not required.)

ORIGINAL

Summary of Events and Information
**62nd DIVISIONAL TRAIN.**

| Place | Date | Hour | | Remarks and references to Appendices |
|---|---|---|---|---|
| MADAGASCAR | 1.2.18 | | Railhead ECURIE Refilling Points for all Corps MADAGASCAR area. Railhead loading 8 A.M. by three Transport for all Corps. Six G.S. Wagons detailed for work with 341 Road Construction Company | A/15 |
| | 2.2.18 | | Railhead and Transport as on 1st | A/15 |
| | 3.2.18 | | do | A/15 |
| | 4.2.18 | | do. 4 Field Kitchens & 4 Water Carts received from 2/6 Duke of Wellington's Regt. | A/15 |
| | 5.2.18 | | Railheads unchanged. Transport detailed as under:- 6 G.S. Wagons for 341 Road Construction Company 8 A.M. 4 do for cutting wood material 3 p.m. 6 do for taking Infantry up the line 3 p.m. 4 Field Kitchens & 2 Water Carts received from 2/5th Y & L. Regt. | A/15 |
| | 6.2.18 | | Railhead and Transport as on 5th. Supplies for 193rd Infantry Brigade for consumption of 8th drawn by 565 Divisional Train from 62nd Divisional Park. 4 Field Kitchens & 2 Water Carts received from 2/6 West Riding Regt. 4 Field Kitchens & 4 Water Carts reported from A.S.C. Base Depot. | A/15 |

H.H. Hughes
LIEUT. COLONEL,
COMMDG. 62nd DIVISIONAL TRAIN.

Army Form C. 2118.

ORIGINAL

# WAR DIARY
## or
## INTELLIGENCE SUMMARY.
(Erase heading not required.)

**62ND DIVISIONAL TRAIN.**

Summary of Events and Information

Instructions regarding War Diaries and Intelligence Summaries are contained in F. S. Regs., Part II. and the Staff Manual respectively. Title pages will be prepared in manuscript.

| Place | Date | Hour | Summary of Events and Information | Remarks and references to Appendices |
|---|---|---|---|---|
| MADAGASCAR. | 7/2/18 | | Railhead and Transport as on 6th Supplies for 187th Brigade Group drawn by M.T. from TINCQUES Railhead (56th Division Park) and dumped at FREVILLERS. 528 Company Canal to FREVILLERS. Railway Post for 187th Brigade HERMIN. Remainder unchanged. 2 Reinforcements. (C.D.M.S. 1 Farrier-Corporal) reported for duty. | H.K. |
| | 8.2.18. | | Railhead unchanged. Transport details as under:- 6 G.S. Wagons of 341 Roads Construction Company to 186th & 187th Brigade Group drawn by H.T. for TINCQUES Railhead (56th Division Park) Supplies for 186th & 187th Brigade Group drawn by H.T. for TINCQUES Railhead and FREVILLERS respectively, and dumped at ROEUX and FREVILLERS. Refilling Points unchanged. | H.K. |
| | 9.2.18 | | Railhead unchanged. Transport details as under:- 6 G.S. Wagons of 341 Road Construction Company 8 A.M. do to take infantry up the line 3 P.M. S.H.Q. and regiments for 186th & 187th Brigade drawn by M.T. drawn for 186th Brigade Group from 186th Brigade Group ROEUX. Remainder unchanged. | H.K. |

H.K. Mullins
LIEUT COLONEL
COMDG. 62ND DIVISIONAL TRAIN.

Army Form C. 2118.

ORIGINAL (3)

# WAR DIARY
## or
## INTELLIGENCE SUMMARY.
*(Erase heading not required.)*

Summary of Events and Information

## 62ND DIVISIONAL TRAIN.

| Place | Date | Hour | Summary of Events and Information | Remarks and references to Appendices |
|---|---|---|---|---|
| MADAGASCAR | 10.4.18 | | Railheads unchanged. Supplies for 187th Brigade Group unchanged. Supplies for 185th/186th Brigade Groups drawn by M.T. from TINCQUES Railhead and Issued at ROCOURT and CHELERS respectively. Refilling Points unchanged. | N.R. |
| MINGOVAL | 12.4.18 | | Railhead TINCQUES. 9 AM. Refilling Points: 187th Bgde Group. ROCOURT. 185th " " CHELERS. 186th " " FRENCUES. 56th Divisional Troops (attached 6th Division) SAVY. 62nd Divisional Troops (attached 56th Division) MADAGASCAR cross roads. Train Headquarters moved to MINGOVAL. 506 Coy ASC to ROCOURT. 511 Company A.S.C. to TINCQUETTE. |  |
|  | 11.4.18 | | No change | N.R. |
|  | 13.4.18 | | No change | N.R. |

H.M. Parker
LIEUT. COLONEL
COMMDG. 62ND DIVISIONAL TRAIN

Army Form C. 2118.

ORIGINAL

# WAR DIARY
## or
## INTELLIGENCE SUMMARY.
(Erase heading not required.)

Instructions regarding War Diaries and Intelligence Summaries are contained in F.S. Regs., Part II. and the Staff Manual respectively. Title pages will be prepared in manuscript.

## 62ND DIVISIONAL TRAIN.

| Place | Date | Hour | Summary of Events and Information | Remarks and references to Appendices |
|---|---|---|---|---|
| MOREUIL | 14.2.18 | | No change. 4 Drivers Reinforcements reported for Base | AAA |
| | 15.2.18 | | 525 Company moved to SAVY. Supplies for 62nd Divisional Troops drawn for TINCQUES by M.T. and sent to at SAVY. | AAA |
| | 16.2.18 | | Railhead unchanged. Refilling Point for 62nd Divisional Troops SAVY (in main arrens 2 M.P. B1 1005) Remainder unchanged. 3 G.S. Wagons for 42. C.A.S. Corps AUBIGNY. Daily detail for transport. 20 for Town Major SAVY. | AAA |
| | 17.2.18 | | No change. | AAA |
| | 18.2.18 | | No change. | AAA |
| | 19.2.18 | | No change. Divisional Troops Refilling Point moved to Sucrerie road SAVY | AAA |
| | 20.2.18 | | No change. | AAA |
| | 21.2.18 | | No change. Capt. H.C. Pearson reported for duty from 24th Divisional Train | AAA |

M.M. Mullingan
LIEUT. COLONEL.
COMMDG. 62ND DIVISIONAL TRAIN

Army Form C. 2118.

ORIGINAL

# WAR DIARY
## or
## INTELLIGENCE SUMMARY.
*(Erase heading not required.)*

### 62ND DIVISIONAL TRAIN.

| Place | Date | Hour | Summary of Events and Information | Remarks and references to Appendices |
|---|---|---|---|---|
| MINGOVAL | 22.2.18 | | No change | |
| | 23.2.18 | | No change | |
| | 24.2.18 | | No change | |
| | 25.2.18 | | No change | |
| | 26.2.18 | | No change | |
| | 27.2.18 | | No change | |
| | 28.2.18 | | 528 Company moved to forward area. Sheet 51 B. A.14.c.7.5. Supplies for 187 Brigade. Good M consumption. Rations for 2nd Brinde by M.T. from 31st Division Park at ECOIVRES and Dumped at ARRAS. SOUCHEZ road at A.20.d.4.6. DDS & T. 1st Army indicates lines of 528 Company A.S.C. 47 SAVY. | |

A. M. ... ...
LIEUT. COLONEL
COMMDG. 62ND DIVISIONAL TRAIN

ORIGINAL.

CONFIDENTIAL.

Vol 15

# WAR DIARY.

OF

## 62ND DIVISIONAL TRAIN.

From :- March. 1st 1918.

To :- March. 31st 1918.

Volume. 15.

Army Form C. 2118.

ORIGINAL

# WAR DIARY
## or
## INTELLIGENCE SUMMARY.
### (Erase heading not required.)
Summary of Events and Information

### 62ND DIVISIONAL TRAIN.

| Place | Date | Hour | Summary of Events and Information | Remarks and references to Appendices |
|---|---|---|---|---|
| MINGOVAL | 1.3.18 | | Railhead – TINCQUES. SAVY. Refilling Points. Divisional Troops. 185th Brigade Group. RECOURT. 186th Brigade Group. CHELERS. 187th Brigade Group. ECURIE. | Appx |
| | 2.3.18 | | Railhead unchanged. Refilling Points unchanged. 517 Company moved to forward area A20.a.7.9. Sheet 51.B. Supplies for 186th Brigade Group for execution March 4th drawn by M.T. from 31st Division Park at ECURIE and dumped at ARRAS-SOUCHEZ road. | Appx |
| | 3.3.18 | | Railhead unchanged. Refilling Point for 186th Brigade Group ARRAS-SOUCHEZ road remainder unchanged. 2 G.S. Wagons (C.T.O) and M.D. lorries detailed for Corps Agricultural Officer MAROEUIL and accompanied by him. Duty detail – 2 G.S. Wagons for Town Major ECOIVRES. 1 for Corps Piggery Rocksicourt | Appx |
| | 4.3.18 | | Railhead ECURIE Refilling Points unchanged. Train Headquarters moved to A20.b.3.4. Sheet 51.B. 516 Company moved to A14.c.9.9. " | Appx |

J.F.W. Kitching Brier
LIEUT. COLONEL,
COMMDG. 62ND DIVISIONAL TRAIN.

Army Form C. 2118.

(2) ORIGINAL

# WAR DIARY
## or
## INTELLIGENCE SUMMARY.
(Erase heading not required.)

Summary of Events and Information: **82ND DIVISIONAL TRAIN.**

| Place | Date | Hour | Summary of Events and Information | Remarks and references to Appendices |
|---|---|---|---|---|
| ECURIE. | 5.3.18 | | Railhead unchanged. Refilling Point for 185th Brigade Group unchanged MADAGASCAR corner. Remainder unchanged. | HH |
| | 6.3.18 | | Railhead unchanged. Refilling Points unchanged. Supplies for Div: Artillery drawn by M.T. from TINCQUES railhead & dumps at ECURIE. Transport details as under:— as on 5.3.18 with addition of 2 G.S. wagons (C.T.) & 4 H.D. horses for Div: Agricultural Officer. 21 "B" Census reports in substitution for 21 "A" Census returns to their units. | HH |
| | 7.3.18 | | Railhead unchanged. Refilling Point for Divisional Troops moved ECURIE. Remainder unchanged. 525 Company moved to ECURIE. Transport details as on 6th with addition of 1 G.S. wagon for Salvage Officer. 1 do Chick Enemy Hut ROCLINCOURT. 1 Limber for Clothing Store ROCLINCOURT. | HH |

H. Williams
LIEUT. COLONEL,
COMMDG. 62ND DIVISIONAL TRAIN.

Army Form C. 2118.

ORIGINAL

# WAR DIARY
## or
## INTELLIGENCE SUMMARY.
(Erase heading not required.)

**62nd DIVISIONAL TRAIN.**

Instructions regarding War Diaries and Intelligence Summaries are contained in F.S. Regs., Part II. and the Staff Manual respectively. Title pages will be prepared in manuscript.

| Place | Date | Hour | Summary of Events and Information | Remarks and references to Appendices |
|---|---|---|---|---|
| ECURIE | 8.3.18 | | Railhead & Refilling Points unchanged. Transport details as on 7th with addition of 2 A.D. horses to Tur Majr Ecoivres. | AF16 |
| | 9.3.18 | | No change. | AF16 |
| | 10.3.18 | | C.Q.M.S. Hamilton 326 Company A.S.C. Sent to report near Office under instructions from D.A.Q. 3rd Echelon. 1 Garrison Staff Sergeant reported from Base. Transport details as on 9th. | AF16 |
| | 11.3.18 | | No change. Reinforcements arrived from Base. 1 Wheeler Staff Sergeant & 3 Drivers. | AF16 |
| | 12.3.18 | | No change. | AF16 |
| | 13.3.18 | | Railhead & Refilling Points unchanged. Transport details as on 12/15 with addition of 5 wagons to 223 Feeds by R.E. | AF16 |
| | 14.3.18 | | No change. | AF16 |
| | 15.3.18 | | No change. | AF16 |
| | 16.3.18 | | No change. | AF16 |

JH Willen Barr
LIEUT. COLONEL
COMMDG. 62ND DIVISIONAL TRAIN.

Army Form C. 2118.

ORIGINAL

# WAR DIARY
## or
## INTELLIGENCE SUMMARY.
(Erase heading not required.)

### 62ND DIVISIONAL TRAIN.
Summary of Events and Information

| Place | Date | Hour | Summary of Events and Information | Remarks and references to Appendices |
|---|---|---|---|---|
| ECOIRIE | 17.3.18 | | Railhead & Refilling Points unchanged. Transport details as on 16th. | A.A.K. |
| | 18.3.18 | | Railhead & Refilling Points unchanged. Lieut. R. J. Pope O/c Supplies 187th Brigade left to report to A.S.C. Base Depôt MARSEILLES. Transport details as on 17th. | A.A.K. |
| | 19.3.18 | | No change. 2/Lieut. T.S.J. Jenkson reported from Base. | A.A.K. |
| | 20.3.18 | | No change. | A.A.K. |
| | 21.3.18 | | No change. | A.A.K. |
| | 22.3.18 | | No change. | A.A.K. |
| | 23.3.18 | | No change. | A.A.K. |
| | 24.3.18 | | Railhead AGNEZ-LEZ-DUISANS. Refilling Points unchanged. Move as follows:- Train Headquarters BERNEVILLE 525 Company do 526 Company do 527 Company Y HUTMENTS ETRUN. 528 Company DUISANS. | A.A.K. |

A. A. Müller Sror
LIEUT. COLONEL,
COMMDG. 62ND DIVISIONAL TRAIN.

Army Form C. 2118.

ORIGINAL

# WAR DIARY
## or
## INTELLIGENCE SUMMARY:
(Erase heading not required.)

### 62ND DIVISIONAL TRAIN.
Summary of Events and Information

Instructions regarding War Diaries and Intelligence Summaries are contained in F.S. Regs., Part II. and the Staff Manual respectively. Title pages will be prepared in manuscript.

| Place | Date | Hour | Summary of Events and Information | Remarks and references to Appendices |
|---|---|---|---|---|
| BERNEVILLE | 25.3.18 | | Railhead unchanged. Refilling Points. Divisional Troops & 185th Brigade Group. BERNEVILLE. 186th & 187th Brigade Groups. ARRAS – ST. POL road. Train Headquarters moved to FONQUEVILLERS. 525 Company to SOUASTRE 526 Company to BIENVILLERS 527 Company to HANNESCAMPS. | Staff |
| FONQUEVILLERS | 26.3.18 | | Railhead unchanged. Refilling Point for Divisional Troops 185th & 186th Brigade Groups POMMIER. 187th Brigade Group. DUISANS. 525 Company moved to HUMBERCAMP. 527 Company to BIENVILLERS. 528 Company to LAHERLIERE. Railhead SAULTY. Refilling points for Divisional Troops HUMBERCAMP. for remainder LAHERLIERE. Train Headquarters moved to HUMBERCAMP. | AAA |
| | 27.3.18 | | | AAA |

J.H. Porter Prest
LIEUT. COLONEL,
COMMDG. 62ND DIVISIONAL TRAIN.

A5834 Wt. W4973/M687 750,000 8/16 D. D. & L. Ltd. Forms/C.2118/13.

Army Form C. 2118.

ORIGINAL

# WAR DIARY
## or
## INTELLIGENCE SUMMARY.
(Erase heading not required.)

### 82ND DIVISIONAL TRAIN.
Summary of Events and Information

| Place | Date | Hour | Summary of Events and Information | Remarks and references to Appendices |
|---|---|---|---|---|
| HOMBLEREAMP | 28.3.18 | | Railhead & Refilling Points unchanged. 41st Div¹. Artillery, 49th Divisional Artillery & 93rd A.F.A. Brigade attached for rations. | Att⁵ |
| | 29.3.18 | | Railhead & Refilling Points unchanged. 4th Australian Infantry Brigade and 15th & 13th Machine Gun Squadrons attached for rations | att⁵ |
| | 30.3.18 | | Railhead WARLINCOURT. 526 & 527 Companies moved to BOIS DE WARNIMONT. 528 Company moved to AUTHIE. Refilling Points for Divisional Troops unchanged. For 185th, 186th & 187th Brigade Groups AUTHIE – THIEVRES road. | att⁵ |
| | 31.3.18 | | Railhead unchanged. Refilling Points for Divisional Troops unchanged. 185th/187th Brigade Groups unchanged. 186th Brigade Group PAS – HENU road. Train Headquarters moved to PAS. 525 Company to SOMASTRE 526 Company to AUTHIE. 527 Company to HENU. | att⁵ |

R.W.M. [signature]
LIEUT. COLONEL,
COMMDG. 82ND DIVISIONAL TRAIN.

O R I G I N A L.　　C O N F I D E N T I A L.

W A R   D I A R Y
of
62ND. DIVISIONAL TRAIN.

From. 1st April 1918.
to. 30th April 1918.

VOLUME: 16.

LIEUT. COLONEL,
COMMDG. 62ND DIVISIONAL TRAIN.

Army Form C. 2118.

ORIGINAL

# WAR DIARY
## or
## INTELLIGENCE SUMMARY

(Erase heading not required.)

62ND DIVISIONAL TRAIN.

| Place | Date | Hour | Summary of Events and Information | Remarks and references to Appendices |
|---|---|---|---|---|
| PAS. | 1.4.18 | | Railhead WARLINCOURT<br>Refilling Points - Divisional Troops - ST-AMAND - SOUASTRE road<br>185th Brigade Group    AUTHIE<br>186th Brigade Group    HENU - PAS road<br>187th Brigade Group    AUTHIE.<br>Supplies drawn from Railhead by M.T. | AHS. |
| | 2.4.18 | | Railhead AUTHIEULE.<br>All units attacks for rations handed over to 37th Division. | AHS. |
| | 3.4.18. | | No change. | AHS. |
| | 4.4.18. | | 525 Company & Divisional Troops R.P. moved to HENU - otherwise no change. | AHS. AHS. |
| | 5.4.18. | | No change. | AHS. |
| | 6.4.18. | | No change. | |
| | 7.4.18. | | Train Headquarters moved to HENU<br>526, 527 & 528 Companies moved to SOUASTRE.<br>Refilling Points. Divisional Troops unchanged<br>185th, 186th & 187th Brigade Groups - HENU - SOUASTRE road. | AHS. |

A.H. Kellyn Jones
LIEUT. COLONEL,
COMMDR. 62nd DIVISIONAL TRAIN.

A5834  Wt. W4973/M687  750,000  8/16  D. D. & L. Ltd.  Forms/C.2118/13.

Army Form C. 2118.

ORIGINAL

# WAR DIARY
or
# INTELLIGENCE SUMMARY.
(Erase heading not required.)

## 62ND DIVISIONAL TRAIN

| Place | Date | Hour | Summary of Events and Information | Remarks and references to Appendices |
|---|---|---|---|---|
| HENU | 8.4.18 | | T/2 Lieut A.R. Young admitted Hospital. | |
| | 9.4.18 | 12 | F.S. Wagons detailed to report HANNESCAMPS at 12 noon. Gr. Divisional Forward Officer | |
| | | 2 | G.S. Wagons detailed for 461st Field Company at FONQUEVILLERS at 8 P.M. | |
| | 10.4.18 | | 6 G.S. Wagons detailed to report to D.F.F D.F.R.O. 12 noon. | |
| | | | 461st Field Company at FONQUEVILLERS 8 P.M. | |
| | | | 526 & 528 Companies moved to HENU | |
| | | | T/Lieut A.P. Gent reports for A.H.T Depot ARROUILLE for duty. | |
| | 11.4.18 | | 2 G.S. Wagons detailed for 461 Field Company at FONQUEVILLERS 8 P.M. | |
| | | | 527 Company moved to HENU | |
| | | | 185th, 186th & 187th Brigade Groups Refilling Points moved to PAS-COUIN road | |
| | 12.4.18 | | Transport as on 11th | |
| | 13.4.18 | | Transport as on 12th. | |
| | | | No change. | |
| | 14.4.18 | | No change. | |
| | 15.4.18 | | 1 Rarsen Captured new present reports for Rear. | |

J.H. Hallgren
LIEUT. COLONEL
Commanding, 62ND DIVISIONAL TRAIN

(3)

Army Form C. 2118.

ORIGINAL

# WAR DIARY
## or
## INTELLIGENCE SUMMARY.
*(Erase heading not required.)*

### 62ND DIVISIONAL TRAIN

Instructions regarding War Diaries and Intelligence Summaries are contained in F.S. Regs., Part II. and the Staff Manual respectively. Title pages will be prepared in manuscript.

| Place | Date | Hour | Summary of Events and Information | Remarks and references to Appendices |
|---|---|---|---|---|
| HENU | 16.4.18 | | No change. | AAA |
| | 17.4.18 | | Train Headquarters, 526, 527 & 528 Companies moved to PAS. | AAA / AAA |
| PAS. | 18.4.18 | | No change. | AAA |
| | 19.4.18 | | T.2/Lieut E.P Goodyear admitted Hospital. 185th, 186th, & 187th Brigade Group Refilling Points moved to PAS. AUTHIE road | AAA / AAA |
| | 20.4.18 | | T/Capt H.C Pearson took over command of 527 Company A.S.C. from Rear to Open. | AAA / AAA / AAA |
| | 21.4.18 | | T.2/Lieut R.G. Bruce admitted Hospital. | AAA / AAA |
| | 22.4.18 | | No change | AAA |
| | 23.4.18 | | No change | AAA |
| | 24.4.18 | | 526 Company A.S.C. moved to LOUVENCOURT. 185th Brigade Group Refilling Point moved to VAUCHELLES. | AAA / AAA |
| | 25.4.18 | | No change | AAA |
| | 26.4.18 | | No change | AAA |
| | 27.4.18 | | No change. | AAA |

[signature]
LIEUT. COLONEL,
COMMDG. 62ND DIVISIONAL TRAIN.

Army Form C. 2118.

ORIGINAL

# WAR DIARY
## or
## INTELLIGENCE SUMMARY.
(Erase heading not required.)

## 62ND DIVISIONAL TRAIN.

Instructions regarding War Diaries and Intelligence Summaries are contained in F. S. Regs., Part II. and the Staff Manual respectively. Title pages will be prepared in manuscript.

| Place | Date | Hour | Summary of Events and Information | Remarks and references to Appendices |
|---|---|---|---|---|
| PAS. | 28.4.18 | | No change | APL |
| | 29.4.18 | | No change | APL |
| | 30.4.18 | | No change | APL |
| | | | Reinforcements. (2 Wheelers Corporals & 12 Drivers) reported from Base. | |

A.R.Mulgrew
LIEUT. COLONEL
COMMDG. 62ND DIVISIONAL TRAIN.

ORIGINAL. CONFIDENTIAL.

Vol 17

# War Diary
## of
## 62ⁿᵈ Divisional Train.

From:- 1ˢᵗ May 1918.
To:- 31ˢᵗ May 1918.

Volume:- 17.

[Signature]
LIEUT. COLONEL
COMMDG. 62ND DIVISIONAL TRAIN.

# WAR DIARY or INTELLIGENCE SUMMARY

Army Form C. 2118.

2nd Divnl Train 62 ORIGINAL

| Place | Date | Hour | Summary of Events and Information | Remarks and references to Appendices |
|---|---|---|---|---|
| PAS | 1.5.18 | | Railhead — AUTHIEULE. Refilling Point — Divisional Troops Group — HENU. 185th Brigade Group — VAUCHELLES. 186th & 187th  to  PAS-AUTHIE Road. Supplies drawn from Railhead by M.T. 1 O.R. reinforcement reported from Base. 1 Hurt Accidn returned to duty from Base | |
| | 2.5.18 | | No change | |
| | 3.5.18 | | No change | |
| | 4.5.18 | | 11 O.R. reinforcements reported from Base | |
| | 5.5.18 | | 2 Hurt Accns evacuated to England through 46 C.C.S. 515 Coy moved from HENU to C.25.a.9.9. | |
| | 6.5.18 | | Divisional Troops Group moved to PAS-AUTHIE area. | |
| | 7.5.18 | | No change | |
| | 8.5.18 | | No change | |
| | 9.5.18 | | No change | |
| | 10.5.18 | | No change | |
| | 11.5.18 | | No change | |
| | 12.5.18 | | No change | |

LIEUT. COLONEL.
COMMDG. 62ND DIVISIONAL TRAIN

**Army Form C. 2118.**

# WAR DIARY
## or
## INTELLIGENCE SUMMARY
(Erase heading not required.)

62nd Divisional Train — 62nd April Train

ORIGINAL

| Place | Date | Hour | Summary of Events and Information | Remarks and references to Appendices |
|---|---|---|---|---|
| PAS. | 13.5.18 | | Divisional Commander inspected Supply Sections of the Train in column of route at AUTHIE | APP/3 |
| | 14.5.18 | | No change | APP/2 |
| | 15.5.18 | | 185th Bde Group Refilling Point moved to PAS — AUTHIE road. 19 Mules drawn from Remount Depôt GEZAINCOURT & distributed to units | APP/11 |
| | 16.5.18 | | 526 Company moved from LOUVENCOURT to PAS. T/Lieut. O'Sullivan reported for duty from Base | APP/12 |
| | 17.5.18 | | No change | APP/12, APP/15 |
| | 18.5.18 | | No change | APP/16 |
| | 19.5.18 | | No change | APP/16 |
| | 20.5.18 | | No change | APP/16 |
| | 21.5.18 | | No change | APP/13 |
| | 22.5.18 | | Gas instruction. S.B. respirators worn by all ranks for 1 hour | APP/10 |
| | 23.5.18 | | do. | APP/8 |
| | 24.5.18 | | do. | APP/8 |
| | 25.5.18 | | do. | APP/15 |
| | 26.5.18 | | 3 O.R.'s proceeded to St. VALERY Rest Camp | APP/13 |

J.H.S. Gee
LIEUT. COLONEL.
COMMDG. 62ND DIVISIONAL TRAIN.

Army Form C. 2118.

ORIGINAL

# WAR DIARY
## or
## INTELLIGENCE SUMMARY.
*(Erase heading not required.)*

**62ND DIVISIONAL TRAIN**

Instructions regarding War Diaries and Intelligence Summaries are contained in F. S. Regs., Part II. and the Staff Manual respectively. Title pages will be prepared in manuscript.

| Place | Date | Hour | Summary of Events and Information | Remarks and references to Appendices |
|---|---|---|---|---|
| PAS. | 26.5.18 | | No change | |
| | 29.5.18 | | No change | |
| | 30.5.18 | | No change | |
| | 31.5.18 | | 4 O.R's reinforcements reported from Base | |

J.H. Williamson
LIEUT. COLONEL
COMMDG. 62ND DIVISIONAL TRAIN.

Original

Confidential

Vol 18

WAR DIARY.
of the
62ⁿᵈ Divisional Train.
VOLUME No. 18
from 1ˢᵗ June 1918
to 30ᵗʰ June 1918.

LIEUT. COLONEL,
COMMDG. 62ᴺᴰ DIVISIONAL TRAIN.

Army Form C. 2118.

# WAR DIARY
## or
## INTELLIGENCE SUMMARY.

(Erase heading not required.)

62nd Div Train    ORIGINAL

| Place | Date | Hour | Summary of Events and Information | Remarks and references to Appendices |
|---|---|---|---|---|
| PHS | 1.6.18 | | Rollans - AUTHIEULE. | |
| | | | Refitting Pants. Dismount. All Ranks Pers. AUTHIE area | AAA |
| | | | Supplies drawn from Rolleans by M.T. | AAA |
| | | | | AAA |
| | 2.6.18 | | No change | |
| | 3.6.18 | | 1st Drawn Reinforcement reported from Base | AAA |
| | 4.6.18 | | No change | |
| | 5.6.18 | | 2/4 Hampshire Regiment joined Division and located at AMPLIER – No Train Transport | AAA |
| | | | 5 Paires H.D. horses detailed to remove their Rations from DOULLENS to AMPLIER. | |
| | | | 20 Remounts drawn for PREMEVILLERS and distributed to units. | AAA |
| | 6.6.18 | | 1/5th Devon Regiment joined Division and located at FANECHON. No Train Transport. | AAA |
| | | | 4 Pairs H.D. horses detailed to remove their Rations from MONDICOURT to FANECHON. | |
| | | | 2nd Drawn Reinforcement reported from Base | |
| | 7.5.18 | | No change | AAA |
| | 6.6.18 | | No change | AAA |
| | 9.6.18 | | No change | AAA |
| | 10.6.18 | | No change | AAA |

[Signed] Lieut Colonel
Commdg. 62nd Division Train

Army Form C. 2118.

62nd Div Train

ORIGINAL

# WAR DIARY
## or
## INTELLIGENCE SUMMARY.
(Erase heading not required.)

Instructions regarding War Diaries and Intelligence Summaries are contained in F. S. Regs., Part II. and the Staff Manual respectively. Title pages will be prepared in manuscript.

| Place | Date | Hour | Summary of Events and Information | Remarks and references to Appendices |
|---|---|---|---|---|
| PAS | 11.6.18 | | Lieut J.A. Spooner 2/5th Y&L (attached) left to report to War Office | |
| | | | 3 O.R. reinforcements reported from Base | |
| | 12.6.18 | | No change | |
| | 13.6.18 | | No change | |
| | 14.6.18 | | 15 G.S. wagons detailed to draw fuel wood for III Corps fuel dump at THIEVRES | |
| | 15.6.18 | | 15 2/Lieut Everitt admitted Hospital | |
| | | | No change | |
| | 16.6.18 | | No change | |
| | 17.6.18 | | 10 G.S. wagons detailed to draw fuel wood for 11 Corps fuel dump at THIEVRES | |
| | 18.6.18 | | No change | |
| | 19.6.18 | | No change | |
| | 20.6.18 | | No change | |
| | 21.6.18 | | S.S.O. left to report to D.D.S.T. Third Army for 2 months course of instruction | |
| | 22.6.18 | | No change | |
| | 23.6.18 | | 2/Lieut. PARROT reported for A.S.C. Base Depot for attachment | |
| | | | 1 Farrier Staff Sergeant + 1 driver casualty reported from Base | |

LIEUT. COLONEL.
COMMDG. 62nd DIVISION TRAIN.

Army Form C. 2118.

WAR DIARY
or
INTELLIGENCE SUMMARY.
(Erase heading not required.)

62nd Div Train
ORIGINAL

| Place | Date | Hour | Summary of Events and Information | Remarks and references to Appendices |
|---|---|---|---|---|
| PKS | 24.6.18 | | Headquarters Company moved to BRUILLE. Divisional Troops supply Point to AMPLIER Church. 526 Company moves to AUTHIEULE. 185th Brigade Refilling Point to FRESCHVILLERS. (A.30.6.2.0). | Apps. |
| | 25.6.18 | | No change | |
| | 26.6.18 | | No change | |
| | 27.6.18 | | No change | |
| | 28.6.18 | | No change | |
| | 29.6.18 | | 14 Mules collected from Remount Dept GEZAINCOURT & distributed to units | |
| | 30.6.18 | | Lieut A.R. Young returned to duty from A.S.C Base Depot. | |

M.W. Bulloughner
LIEUT. COLONEL
COMMDG. 62ND DIVISIONAL TRAIN

ORIGINAL      CONFIDENTIAL.

WAR DIARY.
OF
62ND DIVISIONAL TRAIN.

From: July 1st 1918
To. July 31st 1918.

Volume: 19.

[signature]
LIEUT. COLONEL.
COMMDG. 62ND DIVISIONAL TRAIN.

Army Form C. 2118.

# WAR DIARY
## or
## INTELLIGENCE SUMMARY
(Erase heading not required.)

ORIGINAL

| Place | Date | Hour | Summary of Events and Information | Remarks and references to Appendices |
|---|---|---|---|---|
| PAS | 1/7/17 | | Reached AUTHIEULE. 82ND DIVISIONAL TRAIN. | |
| | | | Artillery Parks. Du Toits AMPLIER Church | |
| | | | 12th Brigade Group AUTHIEULE | |
| | | | 18th 117 at Gough PAS-AUTHIE Road | |
| | 2-7-18 | | No change | |
| | 3-7-17 | | No change | |
| | 4-7-17 | | No change | |
| | 5-7-17 | | No change | |
| | 6-7-17 | | No change | |
| | 7-7-17 | | No change | |
| | 8-7-17 | | No change | |
| | 9-7-17 | | No change | |
| | 10-7-17 | | No change | |
| | 11-7-17 | | No change | |
| | 12-7-17 | | Warning order to move to meet B. Staff of Bar March | |
| | 13-7-17 | | Report Eighth Brigade from DDsr 7. 3rd Army | |
| | 14-7-17 | | No change | |
| | 15-7-17 | | Trans Ko and 27 employing civilians at MONDICOURT | |
| | | | Rest Company at DOULLENS (South) | |
| | | | S2S at do | |
| | | | S73 at do | |
| | 16-7-17 | | at do (NORTH) ) Concentration rendezvous | |
| | 15-7-17 | | Advanced 52 Horses to be consigned to PERCY near PARIS, which now form regular Arg Station | |

Signed
COMMDG. 82ND DIVISIONAL TRAIN
LIEUT. COLONEL

Army Form C. 2118.

ORIGINAL

# WAR DIARY
## or
## INTELLIGENCE SUMMARY.
(Erase heading not required.)

Instructions regarding War Diaries and Intelligence Summaries are contained in F. S. Regs., Part II. and the Staff Manual respectively. Title pages will be prepared in manuscript.

### 62ND DIVISIONAL TRAIN.

| Place | Date | Hour | Summary of Events and Information | Remarks and references to Appendices |
|---|---|---|---|---|
| | 16.7.18 | | Arrived BERCY about 11 a.m. The Train being deplaned for the marching at MONT=REAUX. Train HQ detrained at SOMMESOUS. 525, 526, 527, 528 Companies detrained at ACY-SUR-AUBE. | AHS |
| | 17.7.18 | | Whole Train on the march to area of concentration. | AHS |
| | 18.7.13 | | Railhead JALONS | AHS |
| | 19.7.13 | | 2nd Ech. Refilling Point ROUFFY. 185, 186, 187 Bde at Point on ATHIS-TOURS Road. Train HQ TOURS-SUR-MARNE | AHS |
| | | | 525 " Aufery OIRY |
| | | | 526 " TOURS-SUR-MARNE |
| | | | 527 " ATHIS |
| | | | 528 " BISSEUIL |
| | | | Train Ecr moved with these Pay trucks cart off. 1st Ech. required maint from Trend Depot at JALONS. | |
| FORET de REIMS | 20.7.18 | | Whole Train moved to FORET DE REIMS. | AHS |
| | | | Refilling Point 2nd Ech. Great 185, 187, 1187 Bigade & longs in REIMS-CHAMPILLON Road. 2nd Ech. received all req. 1st Ech required from French Depot at JALONS. | AHS |
| | 21.7.18 | | Owing to counter formation his Ech had to be replaced by Reinf met. Refill did not take place until midnight. | AHS |
| | 22.7.18 | | 2nd Ech. left from Ref. Point 730 A.M. & 1st report received from Trend Depot at JALONS. | AHS |
| | 23.7.18 | | Refilling Points issued. Admirals by of morning came convoy fail owing to absence of roads. the was not possible. It was no more necessary that troops their bivouac at the H of CHAMPILLON HILL making the way up now carried... French Ren. fort on cavaliers. | AHS |

A 5834. Wt. W 4973/M687. 750,000. 8/16. D. D. & L. Ltd. Forms/C.2118/13.

LIEUT. COLONEL
COMMDG. 62ND DIVISIONAL TRAIN.

Army Form C. 2118.

# WAR DIARY
or
## INTELLIGENCE SUMMARY.
(Erase heading not required.)

ORIGINAL

Instructions regarding War Diaries and Intelligence Summaries are contained in F.S. Regs., Part II. and the Staff Manual respectively. Title pages will be prepared in manuscript.

## 62ND DIVISIONAL TRAIN.

| Place | Date | Hour | Summary of Events and Information | Remarks and references to Appendices |
|---|---|---|---|---|
| FORET-A-REIMS | 24.7.18 | | Draft Train band attack. Return to reinforcements arranged to send onwards to 62 Gn/L Brigston Group. | |
| | 25.7.18 | | No change | |
| | 26.7.18 | | No change | |
| | 27.7.18 | | No change | |
| | 27.7.18 | | Information received that Brigadier conflict would on then commanding Br A Gr/a Nº 31 consisting 1 & part Companies consisting 2 Bry Nrs day 3rd Brigade. | |
| | 29.7.18 | | Arrived Railhead OIRY. Got offloading a mistake as reflex arrived at TALONS in morning. | |
| | 30.7.18 | | Railhead TALONS. Arrangements made to take 3 days Train Ration Gathering Point Sp. Br/L. AIGNY 185, 184 and 117 Brigade OIRY. | |
| | 31.7.18 | | From D.G moved to BISSEUIL-PLIVOT Area. 4 & Company moved to FAGNIÈRES. | |

LIEUT. COLONEL.
COMMDG. 62ND DIVISIONAL TRAIN.

CONFIDENTIAL.　　　WR 20

ORIGINAL.

# War Diary

## of

## 62ND Divisional Train

From: 1st August 1918.
To:   31st August 1918.

Volume: 20.

*[signed]*
LIEUT. COLONEL.
COMMDG. 62ND DIVISIONAL TRAIN

Army Form C. 2118.

# WAR DIARY
## or
## INTELLIGENCE SUMMARY.
(Erase heading not required.)

ORIGINAL

| Place | Date | Hour | Summary of Events and Information<br>DIVISIONAL TRAIN. | Remarks and references to Appendices |
|---|---|---|---|---|
| PLIVOT | 1-8-18 | | Railhead     OIRY | |
| | | | Train H.Q.   BISSEUIL-PLIVOT Road | |
| | | | 525 Company  FAGNIÈRES | |
| | | | 526 }<br>527 } Companies BISSEUIL-PLIVOT Road<br>528 } | |
| | | | Rallying Point. Div Jonction CHÂLONS | |
| | | | 135 Brigade Group  OIRY | |
| | | | 136       " " | |
| | | | 137       " " | |
| | 2-8-18 | | 525 Company entrained at CHÂLONS | AJR |
| | | | Rallying Point.  136 Brigade Group   VERTUS | |
| | | |                  136       "       OIRY | |
| | | |                  137       "       ÉPERNAY | |
| | 3-8-18 | | No change | AJR |
| | 4-8-18 | | Train H.Q. entrained at ÉPERNAY | AJR |
| | | | 526  Coy   "  "   VERTUS | |
| | | | 527  "     "  "   OIRY | |
| | | | 528  "     "  "   ÉPERNAY | |
| | | | 525  "     detrained at DOULLENS | |

**Army Form C. 2118.**

# WAR DIARY
## or
## INTELLIGENCE SUMMARY.
*(Erase heading not required.)*

ORIGINAL

| Place | Date | Hour | Summary of Events and Information | Remarks and references to Appendices |
|---|---|---|---|---|
| PAS | 1-8-18 | | Railhead AUTHEULE DOULLENS | |
| | | | From HQ to railhead at CANDAS | |
| | | | 521 Coy " " DOULLENS | |
| | | | 522 Coy " " MONDICOURT | |
| | | | 527 Coy " " | |
| | | | Refilling Point Div. Inf. Bois-DU-WARNIMONT | |
| | 2-8-18 | | From HQ PAS | |
| | | | 521 Coy LOUVENCOURT | |
| | | | 527 Coy PAS-AUTHIE road | |
| | | | 528 Coy PAS | |
| | | | Refilling Point 173 Bgde Group VAUCHELLES | |
| | | | " 174 " PAS-AUTHIE Rd | |
| | | | " 175 " " | |
| | 3-8-18 | | No change | |
| | | | 16 Coys to Dump | |
| | | | 2 MG Coys to field Amb hospital | |
| | | | 10 Bakers 3 Supplement moved to Place 9 men | |
| | | | 1 Supp'y return rejoined from Base | |
| | 4-8-18 | | No change | |

GORNDG. 62ND DIVISIONAL TRAIN.

A 5834  Wt. W4973/M687  750,000  8/16  D. D. & L. Ltd.  Forms/C.2118/13.

Army Form C. 2118.

# WAR DIARY
## or
## INTELLIGENCE SUMMARY.
(Erase heading not required.)

ORIGINAL

Instructions regarding War Diaries and Intelligence Summaries are contained in F.S. Regs., Part II. and the Staff Manual respectively. Title pages will be prepared in manuscript.

Summary of Events and Information
52ND DIVISIONAL TRAIN.

| Place | Date | Hour | Summary of Events and Information | Remarks and references to Appendices |
|---|---|---|---|---|
| PAS | 10-8-18 | | No change | AF/N2 |
| | 11-8-18 | | 14 Reinforcements arrived from Base. Remounts distributed to Units by 525 Coy. (LD 48. HD 24) | AF/N2 AF/N2 |
| | 12-8-18 | | No change | AF/N2 |
| | 13-8-18 | | No change | AF/N2 |
| | 14-8-18 | | No change | AF/N2 |
| | | | 1 S.S.M. Reinforcement rejoined from Base. Remounts distributed to Units G 525 Coy. (R.C. Mc? P L) | |
| | 15-8-18 | | No change | AF/N2 |
| | 16-8-18 | | 1 Sgt rejoined from Base | AF/N2 |
| | | | Train HQ moved to AUTHIE | AF/N2 |
| AUTHIE | 17-8-18 | | Roselage. 1 Corp.? A nurse returned to Base. | AF/N2 |
| | 18-8-18 | | No change | AF/N2 |
| | 19-8-18 | | From HQ moved to PAS 526 Coy " HUMBERCOURT 527 " " SAULTY 528 " " SUS-ST-LEGER 2.O.R. Reinforcements rejoined from Base | AF/N2 |

[Signed]
Lieut Colonel,
COMMDG. 52ND DIVISIONAL TRAIN.

Army Form C. 2118.

# WAR DIARY
## or
## INTELLIGENCE SUMMARY.
*(Erase heading not required.)*

ORIGINAL

62nd DIVISIONAL TRAIN.

| Place | Date | Hour | Summary of Events and Information | Remarks and references to Appendices |
|---|---|---|---|---|
| PAS | 20-8-18 | | Railhead WARLINCOURT. | |
| | | | Refilling Points | |
| | | | 185 Bgde Group } BELLE VUE CORNER | |
| | | | 186   " } | |
| | | | 187   " } COULLEMONT-COUTURELLE Road | AFN |
| | 21-8-18 | | Train HQ moved to BAVINCOURT-BARLY Road | |
| | | | 526 Coy LA CAUCHIE | |
| | | | 527 " SAULTY | |
| | | | 528 " SAULTY | |
| | | | Train HQ moved to ORVILLE | |
| | | | 526 Coy VAUCHELLES | |
| | | | 527 " PAS | |
| | | | 528 " BOIS de WARNIMONT | |
| | | | Refilling Point | |
| | | | 185 Bgde Group } BELLE VUE CORNER | |
| | | | 186 " do | |
| | | | 187 " } SAULTY-COUTURELLE Road | AFN |
| ORVILLE | 22-8-18 | | Train HQ moved to PAS | |
| | | | 526 " ST AMAND | |
| | | | 527 " ST AMAND | |
| | | | 528 " Bois de St AMAND | |
| | | | Refilling Point | |
| | | | 185 Bde Group } ORVILLE-THIEVRES Road | |
| | | | 186 " do | |
| | | | 187 " } | AFN |

LIEUT. COLONEL,
COMMDG. 62nd DIVISIONAL TRAIN.

# WAR DIARY
## or
## INTELLIGENCE SUMMARY.
*(Erase heading not required.)*

Army Form C. 2118.

**62ND DIVISIONAL TRAIN.**

| Place | Date | Hour | Summary of Events and Information | Remarks and references to Appendices |
|---|---|---|---|---|
| PAS | 23rd Nov | | Railhead AUTHIEULE | |
| | | | 526 Coy } Moved to LA BAZIQUE | |
| | | | 527 Coy } | |
| | | | 528 Coy } | |
| | | | Refilling Point | |
| | | | 525 Coy at Gonk  VAUCHELLES | |
| | | | 526   „    „   PAS-AUTHIE Rd | |
| | | | 527   „    „        „ | |
| | 24/11/16 | | Refilling Point moved to POMMIER-BIENVILLERS Road | JHL |
| | | | 525 Coy      „          TOUTENCOURT | |
| | | | 526 Coy      „          MONCHY-au-BOIS | |
| | | | 527 Coy      „             „ | |
| | | | 528 Coy      „          MONCHY-BIENVILLERS Road | |
| | | | Refilling Point 525 Brigade Gonk } MONCHY-ADINFER Road | |
| | | |               „      526   „     „  | |
| | | |               „      527   „     „  | |
| | 25/11/16 | | Railhead SAULTY | |
| | | | 525 Coy and Div Hqrs Refilling Gonk  HARPONVILLE | JHL |

Lt Col
Commdg. 62nd Divisional Train.

Army Form C. 2118.

# WAR DIARY
## or
## INTELLIGENCE SUMMARY.
(Erase heading not required.)

ORIGINAL

Instructions regarding War Diaries and Intelligence Summaries are contained in F. S. Regs., Part II. and the Staff Manual respectively. Title pages will be prepared in manuscript.

| Place | Date | Hour | Summary of Events and Information | Remarks and references to Appendices |
|---|---|---|---|---|
| BIENVILLERS | | | 52ND DIVISIONAL TRAIN. | |
| | 26.7.18 | | From M.P. moved to BIENVILLERS | AWS |
| | 27.7.18 | | 525 Coy and Bn.H.Qrs. Supplying Coris HEDAUVILLE 2 O.R. reinforcements reported from Base | AWS AWS AWS AWS |
| | 23.7.18 | | 523 Horse Coy moved to AVELUY Bn. H.Qrs. Supplying Coris ALBERT | |
| | 29.7.18 | | Railhead BOISLEUX AU MONT | |
| | | | No change | |
| | 30.8.18 | | 525 Company and Bn. H.Qrs. Supplying Coris moved to BAZENTIN. | |
| | | | 526 Coy } 527 Coy } moved to DOUCHY-lez-Ayette. 528 Coy } | |
| | | | Supplying Corps | |
| | | | 185 Coy's Group } 176 do } DOUCHY - BOIRY Road. 187 do } | |
| | | | Railhead BOYELLES | AWS |
| | 31.8.18 | | 1 O.R. and 1 Extra reinforcement reported from Base 1 Category A man returned to Base | AWS |

[Signature]
LIEUT. COLONEL,
COMMDG. 52ND DIVISIONAL TRAIN.

Original. Confidential. WD 21

War Diary
of the
62ⁿᵈ Divisional Train
from 1.9.18.
to 30.9.18.

VOLUME 21.

[signature]
LIEUT. COLONEL,
COMMDG. 62ND DIVISIONAL TRAIN.

Army Form C. 2118.

ORIGINAL 1

# WAR DIARY
## or
## INTELLIGENCE SUMMARY.
(Erase heading not required.)

| Place | Date | Hour | Summary of Events and Information | Remarks and references to Appendices |
|---|---|---|---|---|
| COURCELLES | 1.9.18 | | 62nd Divisional Train | |
| | | | Railhead BOYELLES | |
| | | | Train Headquarters moved from BIENVILLERS to COURCELLES (A 20 a 35) | Apps.1 |
| | | | 525 Company BAZENTIN LE PETIT | App.1. |
| | | | 526, 527 & 528 Companies DOUETTY 'LES AYETTE | App.1. |
| | | | Refilling Points. | |
| | | | Divisional Troops BAZENTIN LE PETIT. | App.2 |
| | | | 185, 186, 187 Brigade Groups DOUETTY - BOIRY ST RICHTRUDE roads. | App.2. |
| | 2.9.18 | | No change | App.2. |
| | 3.9.18 | | No change | App.2. |
| | 4.9.16. | | 526, 527 and 528 Companies moved to ERVILLERS | |
| | | | Refilling Points for 3 Brigade Groups moved to ERVILLERS - HAMELINCOURT road | |
| | 5.9.18 | | No change | |
| | 6.9.18 | | No change | |
| | 7.9.18 | | 525 Company moved to ARLAINZEVELLE | |
| | | | Refilling Point for Divisional Troops moved to COURCELLES - ARLAINZEVELLE road | |
| | 8.9.18 | | No change | |

A. H. Kilner Jones.
LIEUT. COLONEL,
COMMDG. 62ND DIVISIONAL TRAIN.

Army Form C. 2118.

# WAR DIARY
## or
## INTELLIGENCE SUMMARY.

(Erase heading not required.)

ORIGINAL  62nd Divisional Train

| Place | Date | Hour | Summary of Events and Information | Remarks and references to Appendices |
|---|---|---|---|---|
| COURCELLES | 9.9.18 | | 14 L.D. and 8 H.D. remounts drawn from ROYELLES. | AHHS |
| | 10.9.18 | | 525 Company moved to FREMICOURT. Refilling Point for Divisional Troops FREMICOURT. 526, 527 & 528 Companies moved to HAPLINCOURT - BEUGNY road. Refilling Points for 3 Brigade Groups HAPLINCOURT - BEUGNY road. Train Headquarters moved to HAPLINCOURT - BEUGNY road. | AHHS AHHS AHHS |
| HAPLINCOURT | 11.9.18 | | No change | |
| | 12.9.18 | | No change | |
| | 13.9.18 | | No change | |
| | 14.9.18 | | No change | |
| | 15.9.18 | | Train Headquarters moved to COURCELLES. 526, 527 & 528 Companies moved to ERVILLERS. Refilling Points for 3 Brigade Groups ERVILLERS - HAMELINCOURT road. | AHHS |
| COURCELLES | 16.9.18 | | No change | AHHS |
| | 17.9.18 | | No change | AHHS |
| | 18.9.18 | | No change | AHHS |
| | 19.9.18 | | No change | AHHS |

[signature]
LIEUT-COLONEL
COMMDG. 62ND DIVISIONAL TRAIN

Army Form C. 2118.

# WAR DIARY
## or
## INTELLIGENCE SUMMARY.
(Erase heading not required.)

62nd Divisional Train     ORIGINAL

Instructions regarding War Diaries and Intelligence Summaries are contained in F. S. Regs., Part II. and the Staff Manual respectively. Title pages will be prepared in manuscript.

| Place | Date | Hour | Summary of Events and Information | Remarks and references to Appendices |
|---|---|---|---|---|
| COURCELLES | 20.9.18 | | Supplies drawn from Railhead by H.T. | |
| | 21.9.18 | | G.H.D. and B.M. renewals drawn from ACHIET-LE-GRAND | |
| | 22.9.18 | | No change | |
| | 23.9.18 | | No change | |
| | 24.9.18 | | No change | |
| | 25.9.18 | | No change | |
| BEAUMETZ | 26.9.18 | | Train Headquarters moved to BEAUMETZ-LES-CAMBRAI. 526, 527 & 528 Companies moved to HAPLINCOURT - BEUGNY road. Refilling Point for 3 Brigade Groups HAPLINCOURT - BEUGNY road. 525 Company moved to RUYAUCOURT. Refilling Point for Divisional Troops P.10.a.8.7. (Sheet 57 C) Railhead VELU | |
| | 28.9.18 | | 526 & 528 Companies moved to P.4.a (central) Sheet 57 C. 527 Company moved to P.3.c.9.7. Sheet 57 S. No change | |
| | 29.9.18 | | Train Headquarters moved to HAVRINCOURT Refilling Point to FLESQUIERES. (K.23.d.3.9) | |
| HAVRINCOURT | 30.9.18 | | 525 Company & Divisional Troops Refilling Point | |

Lt. Colonel,
Commdg. 62nd Divisional Train.

Confidential     Original     No. 22

WAR DIARY
of the
62ND DIVISIONAL TRAIN.

from 1.10.18.
to 31.10.18.

VOLUME. 22.

LIEUT. COLONEL,
COMMDG. 62ND DIVISIONAL TRAIN.

Army Form C. 2118.

# WAR DIARY
## or
## INTELLIGENCE SUMMARY.
(Erase heading not required.)

ORIGINAL

Instructions regarding War Diaries and Intelligence Summaries are contained in F. S. Regs., Part II. and the Staff Manual respectively. Title pages will be prepared in manuscript.

82ND DIVISIONAL TRAIN

| Place | Date | Hour | Summary of Events and Information | Remarks and references to Appendices |
|---|---|---|---|---|
| HAVRINCOURT | 1-10-18 | | Routhead HAVRINCOURT | |
| | | | Train H.Q. K.22 c.5.4 | |
| | | | 525 Company K.23 a.3.9 | |
| | | | 526 do P.4 a central | |
| | | | 527 do P.3 c.9.7 | |
| | | | 528 do P.4 a central | |
| | | | Refilling Point Div. Infn. K.23 a.3.9 | |
| | | | 126 Brigade Group R.P. | |
| | | | 186 do ) P.4 c.6.0 | |
| | | | 187 do ) | |
| | | | 16 Remounts (mules) drawn from FREMICOURT | A.16 |
| | 2-10-18 | | Remounts distributed | A.16 |
| | 3-6-18 | | 2 N.T. Reinforcements arrived from Base | A.16 |
| | 4-10-18 | | do | A.16 |

A.N. McLeod
LIEUT. COLONEL,
COMMDG. 82ND DIVISIONAL TRAIN.

# WAR DIARY
## or
## INTELLIGENCE SUMMARY.

(Erase heading not required.)

Army Form C. 2118.

ORIGINAL

## 62ND DIVISIONAL TRAIN

| Place | Date | Hour | Summary of Events and Information | Remarks and references to Appendices |
|---|---|---|---|---|
| HAVRINCOURT | 5/10/18 | | Railhead cleared by Hors transport | AHK |
| | 6-10-18 | | No change | AHK |
| | 7-10-18 | | do | AHK |
| | 8-10-18 | | Railhead cleared by trains | AHK |
| | | | 3R. 20 Mules 7 H.D. 10 veh. Remounts drawn from VELU. | |
| | 9-10-18 | | Remounts distributed | AHK |
| | 10-10-18 | | Sections MASNIERES 3an. H.Q. moved to L.27 d 9.0. All Employment moved to MARCOING | AHK |
| | | | Refilling point for all Supply L.29.a. | |
| | | | Railhead MASNIERES | |
| | 11-10-18 | | From B/O moved to H.19. d.5.0. | |
| | | | 625 Company moved to H.19. c.5.3 | |
| | | | 626 do do H.19. c.9.0. | |
| | | | 627 do do H.19. Z.9.0. | |
| | | | 628 do do H.19. Z.6.3 | |
| | | | All refilling taking place in SERANVILLERS. | |

[signature]
LIEUT. COLONEL
COMMDG. 62ND DIVISIONAL TRAIN.

Army Form C. 2118.

# WAR DIARY
## or
## INTELLIGENCE SUMMARY.
(Erase heading not required.)

ORIGINAL

Instructions regarding War Diaries and Intelligence Summaries are contained in F. S. Regs., Part II. and the Staff Manual respectively. Title pages will be prepared in manuscript.

62ND DIVISIONAL TRAIN

| Place | Date | Hour | Summary of Events and Information | Remarks and references to Appendices |
|---|---|---|---|---|
| | 12-10-18 | | 525 Company moved to I.9.c.3.4. | |
| | | | Divisional Dumps refilling point FONTAINE-AU-PIRE | |
| | | | From H.Q moved to H.12.c.8.7. | |
| CATTANIERES | 13-10-18 | | 526 & 527 Companies to CATTANIERES | |
| | | | 186 & 185 Brigade dumps H.12.L.3.9. | |
| | 14-10-18 | | 525 Company moved to C.25.c.3.5. | |
| | | | Divisional Packs refilling point C.25.c.3.3. | |
| | 15-10-18 | | Railhead CAMBRAI ANNEXE. | |
| | 16-10-18 | | No change | |
| | 17-10-18 | | Railhead FREMICOURT (owing to breakdown on railway) | |
| | | | 528 Company moved to CATTANIERES | |
| | | | 187 Brigade refilling point moved to H.12.L.3.9. | |
| | | | 3 Reinforcements arrived from Base. | |
| | 18-10-18 | | Railhead CAMBRAI ANNEXE. | |
| | 19-10-18 | | No change. | |

[signature]
LIEUT. COLONEL,
COMMDG. 62ND DIVISIONAL TRAIN.

Army Form C. 2118.

WAR DIARY
or
INTELLIGENCE SUMMARY.
(Erase heading not required.)

ORIGINAL

Instructions regarding War Diaries and Intelligence Summaries are contained in F. S. Regs., Part II. and the Staff Manual respectively. Title pages will be prepared in manuscript.

62ND DIVISIONAL TRAIN

| Place | Date | Hour | Summary of Events and Information | Remarks and references to Appendices |
|---|---|---|---|---|
| BÉVILLERS | 20-10-18 | | Reached AVOIGNT | |
| | | | From H.Q moved to BÉVILLERS | |
| | | | 526, 527, 528 Companies moved to WAMBAIX | |
| | 21-10-18 | | 8 Remounts (riding) drawn by 528 Company | A/1 |
| | | | Remounts distributed | A/2 |
| | 22-10-18 | | No change | A/3 |
| | 23-10-18 | | No change | A/4 |
| | 24-10-18 | | 526, 527, 528 Companies moved to BÉVILLERS | A/5 |
| | | | 185-186-187 Brigade refilling point C.32.c.7.6 | |
| | | | Div. Troops " " E.1.c.4.3 | |
| | | | 525 Company moved to E.1.c.3 (SOLESMES) | |
| | 25-10-18 | | No change | A/6 |
| | 26-10-18 | | No change | A/7 |
| | 27-10-18 | | 2 Reinforcements reported from Base | A/8 |
| | 28-10-18 | | No change | A/9 |

[signature]
LIEUT. COLONEL
COMMDG. 62ND DIVISIONAL TRAIN.

T.134. Wt. W708—776. 500000. 4/15. Sir J. C. & S.

Army Form C. 2118.

# WAR DIARY
## or
## INTELLIGENCE SUMMARY.
(Erase heading not required.)

ORIGINAL

Instructions regarding War Diaries and Intelligence Summaries are contained in F. S. Regs., Part II. and the Staff Manual respectively. Title pages will be prepared in manuscript.

62ND DIVISIONAL TRAIN.

| Place | Date | Hour | Summary of Events and Information | Remarks and references to Appendices |
|---|---|---|---|---|
| BEVILLERS | 29-10-18 | | No change | |
| | 30-10-18 | | No change | |
| | 31-10-18 | | Train HQ march to QUIEVY | |
| | | | 526, 527, 528 Companies march to QUIEVY | |
| | | | 525 ⎫ | |
| | | | 526 ⎬ Brigade Coys. refilling points D.16.c.3.4. | |
| | | | 527 ⎭ | |

LIEUT. COLONEL,
COMMDG. 62ND DIVISIONAL TRAIN.

Original. Confidential. Vol 23

# WAR DIARY
## of the
### 62ND DIVISIONAL TRAIN.

from 1.11.18.
to 30.11.18.

## VOLUME 23.

[signature]
LIEUT. COLONEL,
COMMDG. 62ND DIVISIONAL TRAIN.

Army Form C. 2118.

# WAR DIARY
## or
## INTELLIGENCE SUMMARY.
(Erase heading not required.)

ORIGINAL

62ND DIVISIONAL TRAIN. Summary of Events and Information

| Place | Date | Hour | Summary of Events and Information | Remarks and references to Appendices |
|---|---|---|---|---|
| QUIEVY | 1-11-18 | | Railhead AWOIGNT. | |
| | | | Train Headquarters QUIEVY | |
| | | | 525 Company E1 c1.3. (Ma1573) | |
| | | | 526 } | |
| | | | 527 } Companies QUIEVY. | |
| | | | 528 } | |
| | | | Refilling front | |
| | | | Divisional Troops E1c 1.3. | |
| | | | 185 } | |
| | | | 186 } Brigade Groups D16c 3.4. | AHS |
| 2-11-18 | | | One day's iron rations and one man's Division from CAUDRY and taken to ESCARMAIN and were taken. according to instructions from Brig. D. to have them drawn from MARCOING but were not available there. | AHS |
| 3-11-18 | | | 527 & 528 Companies moved to SOLESMES. | |
| | | | Train HQrs, 527 & 528 Companies moved to ROMERIES | AHS |
| 4-11-18 | | | 526 Company moved to RUESMES | |
| | | | Refilling points | |
| | | | Divisional Troops RUESMES-BEAUDIGNIES ROAD. | |
| | | | 185 } | |
| | | | 186 } Brigade Groups RUESNES- VERTAIN ROAD. | AHS |
| | | | 187 } | |

A.H.S.
LIEUT. COLONEL.
COMMDG. 62ND DIVISIONAL TRAIN.

Army Form C. 2118.

# WAR DIARY
## or
## INTELLIGENCE SUMMARY.
(Erase heading not required.)

ORIGINAL

2ND DIVISIONAL TRAIN. Summary of Events and Information

| Place | Date | Hour | Summary of Events and Information | Remarks and references to Appendices |
|---|---|---|---|---|
| RUESNES | 5-11-18 | | Train H.Q. 526, 527 & 528 Companies marched RUESNES. | AHB |
| | | | 525 Company marched to FRASNOY | |
| | | | Refilling Point | |
| | | | Divisional Troops FRASNOY | |
| | 6-11-18 | | 525 ⎫ | |
| | | | 526 ⎬ Brigade Groups RUESNES-BERMERAIN ROAD. | AHB |
| | | | 527 ⎭ | |
| | | | Railhead CAMBRAI ANNEXE | AHB |
| | | | 525 ⎫ | |
| | | | 526 ⎬ Brigade Groups Refilling Point M.14.d.77. (Sheet 51) | |
| | 7-11-18 | | 527 ⎭ | |
| | | | 528 Company moved to ORSINVAL | |
| | | | Railhead SOLESMES. | |
| | 8-11-18 | | Train H.Q. 526, 527 & 528 Companies moved to GOMMEGNIES | AHB |
| | | | 525 " " " " OBIES | |
| | | | Refilling Point | |
| | | | Divisional Troops. M.4.z.1.5. (Sheet 51). | |
| | | | 525 ⎫ | |
| | | | 526 ⎬ Brigade Groups MARKET SQUARE GOMMEGNIES. | |
| | | | 527 ⎭ | |

A. H. Allan Bart
LIEUT. COLONEL.
COMMDG. 62ND DIVISIONAL TRAIN.

Army Form C. 2118.

# WAR DIARY
## or
## INTELLIGENCE SUMMARY.
(Erase heading not required.)

OR/3/1/82

Instructions regarding War Diaries and Intelligence Summaries are contained in F. S. Regs., Part II. and the Staff Manual respectively. Title pages will be prepared in manuscript.

## 62ND DIVISIONAL TRAIN.

| Place | Date | Hour | Summary of Events and Information | Remarks and references to Appendices |
|---|---|---|---|---|
| OBIES | 9-11-18 | | Train 7.0 521, 527 & 523 Companies moved to OBIES. 525 Company moved to L'ERMITAGE. Refilling points Divisional Troops N & C Central. | A.H.S. |
| | 10-11-18 | | 185, 186, 187 } Brigade Groups GOMMEGNIES. Train HQ and all Companies moved to NEUF MESNIL. Refilling point. Divisional Troops. P 10 c 8.r. (Sheet 51) | A.H.S. |
| NEUF MESNIL | 11-11-18 | | 185, 186, 187 } Brigade Group P 20 a.5.3. (Sheet 51). 185, 186, 187 } Brigade Groups Refilling points. P a Central. Hostilities ceased at 11 a.m. | A.H.S. |
| | 12-11-18 | | No change. | A.H.S. |
| | 13-11-18 | | 1 day Hard ration convoy from BAVAY by tank transport. Rum ration drawn from SOLESMES. A.S.T. established at BAVAI. | A.H.S. |

A.H.Murray
LIEUT. COLONEL
COMMDG. 62nd DIVISIONAL TRAIN.

Army Form C. 2118.

# WAR DIARY
## or
## INTELLIGENCE SUMMARY

(Erase heading not required.)

ORIGINAL

## 82ND DIVISIONAL TRAIN.

| Place | Date | Hour | Summary of Events and Information | Remarks and references to Appendices |
|---|---|---|---|---|
| NEUF-MESNIL | 14-11-18 | | Remounts drawn from CAUDRY. Perlus 2, Roules 13, HD 11, Pack 2. | AHS |
| | 15-11-18 | | No change | AHS |
| | 16-11-18 | | Train HQ moved to SOUS-LE-BOIS | AHS |
| | | | 525 Company to ROUSIES | |
| | | | 526 " " COLLERET | |
| | | | Refitting horses Div Batteries ROUSIES | AHS |
| | | | 135 Brigade Group COLLERET | |
| | | | 31 H.D Div drawn from 20th Division | |
| SOUS-LE-BOIS | 17-11-18 | | No change | |
| | 18-11-18 | | Train HQ moved to COUSOLRE | AHS |
| | | | 525 Company " " MONTIGNIES-ST-CHRISTOPHE | |
| | | | 527 Company " " COUSOLRE | |
| | | | 528 Company " " FERRIERE-LA-GRANDE | |
| | | | Refitting horses | |
| | | | 125 Brigade Group MONTIGNIES | |
| | | | 176 Brigade Group COUSOLRE | |
| | | | 187 Brigade Group FERRIERE-LA-GRANDE | |

JHPowLugCres
LIEUT. COLONEL
COMMDG. 82ND DIVISIONAL TRAIN.

Army Form C. 2118.

# WAR DIARY
## or
## INTELLIGENCE SUMMARY.
*(Erase heading not required.)*

CR/1244/4

62ND DIVISIONAL TRAIN

| Place | Date | Hour | Summary of Events and Information | Remarks and references to Appendices |
|---|---|---|---|---|
| SOUS-LE-BOIS | 19/11/17 | | Train H.Q. and 527 Company moved to LABORNE | |
| | | | 525 Company to FONTAINE-HAUTE | |
| | | | 526 Company to HAM-SUR-HEURE | |
| | | | 528 Company to MONTIGNIES-ST-CHRISTOPHE | |
| | | | Refilling Points | |
| | | | Div. Troops. | FONTAINE-HAUTE |
| | | | 185 Brigade Group | HAM-SUR-HEURE |
| | | | 186 " " | LABORNE |
| | | | 187 " " | MONTIGNIES-ST-CHRISTOPHE |
| | 20/11/17 | | Train H.Q. and 527 Company moved to SOMZEE | |
| | | | 525 Company to BERSÉE | |
| | | | 526 Company to FROMIÉE | |
| | | | 528 Company to HAM-SUR-HEURE. Supplies dumped under VI Corps instructions at CROZÉE. No supplies arrived at R.P.s to-day | |
| | | | Refilling Points | |
| | | | Div. Troops. | SOMZEE |
| | | | 185 Brigade Group | GERPINNES |
| | | | 186 " " | SOMZEE |
| | | | 187 " " | MARBAIX |

LIEUT. COLONEL
COMDG. 62ND DIVISIONAL TRAIN

Army Form C. 2118.

ORIGINAL

# WAR DIARY
## or
## INTELLIGENCE SUMMARY.
(Erase heading not required.)

Instructions regarding War Diaries and Intelligence Summaries are contained in F. S. Regs., Part II. and the Staff Manual respectively. Title pages will be prepared in manuscript.

## 62ND DIVISIONAL TRAIN.

| Place | Date | Hour | Summary of Events and Information | Remarks and references to Appendices |
|---|---|---|---|---|
| SOMZEE | 21-11-18 | | 526 Coy HQ moved to COURDINNES. Supplies brought forward to R.P's from GOZEE by 8 g.s.f. lorries attached to formations. Supplies 24 hours late. | A.H.S |
| | 22-11-18 | | 523 Coy HQ moved to MARBAIX A.S.P. moved forward to GIVRY. No change | A.H.S A.H.S |
| | 23-11-18 | | | |
| | 24-11-18 | | Train HQ moved to NOUECHAMPS 525 Company to MYMIEE 526 " " GRAUX 527 " " BIESMIES 528 " " JONCRET Reserve Park to SOMZEE Divisional Baths GERTRINNES 185 Brigade Group SOMZEE 176 " " SOMZEE 187 " " BERTRANSART. | A.H.S |

[signature]
LIEUT. COLONEL.
COMMDG. 62ND DIVISIONAL TRAIN.

Army Form C. 2118.

# WAR DIARY
## or
## INTELLIGENCE SUMMARY.
*(Erase heading not required.)*

CT/61/NM2

62ND DIVISIONAL TRAIN. Summary of Events and Information

| Place | Date | Hour | Summary of Events and Information | Remarks and references to Appendices |
|---|---|---|---|---|
| DENÉE | 23/11/18 | | 3am H.Q moved to DENÉE | |
| | | | 525 Coy Supply to BIESMERÉE | |
| | | | 526 do do YVOIR | |
| | | | 527 do do ST GERARD | |
| | | | 528 do do METTET | |
| | | | Refilling Points Div Troops GERPINNES | |
| | | | 185 Bde Group GRAUX | |
| | | | 186 do DIESMES | |
| | | | 187 do GERPINNES | |
| | | | Owing to lateness of arrival of supplies nails of 185th & 186th Brigade Groups did not receive supplies in time for issue | N.T.S |
| | 25/11/18 | | Train H.Q & 527 Coy moved to EURÉ HAILLES | |
| | | | 526 Coy Supply to BIRON | |
| | | | 527 do do | |
| | | | 528 do do WARNANT | |
| | | | Refilling Points | |
| | | | Div Troops BIESMERÉE | |
| | | | 185 Brigade Group SPONTINE | |
| | | | 186 do EURE HAILLES - PURNODE ROAD | |
| | | | 187 do BIOUL | |
| | | | Two days rations requisitioned from CHARLEROI. Ten motor lorries were requested for to practicable at Rosteleal. This was necessary owing to distance of R.P.'s from A.S.P at GIVRY and impossibility of getting lorries forward with supplies from GIVRY. | N.T.S |

A.J. McArthur LIEUT. COLONEL
COMMDG. 62nd. DIVISIONAL TRAIN.

Army Form C. 2118.

# WAR DIARY
## or
## INTELLIGENCE SUMMARY.
(Erase heading not required.)

ORIGINAL

### 62ND DIVISIONAL TRAIN.

| Place | Date | Hour | Summary of Events and Information | Remarks and references to Appendices |
|---|---|---|---|---|
| CORBION | 27/11/18 | | Bar. H.Q and 527 Company arrived to CORBION | |
| | | | 525 Company to GEMMECHENNE | |
| | | | 526 " " YCHIPPE | |
| | | | 528 " " CROIX | |
| | | | Refilling Points | |
| | | | Divisional Troops GEMMECHENNE | |
| | | | 185th Brigade Group CHAPOIS | |
| | | | 187 " " CORBION | |
| | | | 186 " " ACHENE | M.T.S. |
| | 28/11/18 | | Reached DINANT | M.T.S. |
| | | | 187th Brigade Group & Artillery moved to ACHENE | |
| | | | Owing to non arrival of M.S.P cars were requisitioned locally | |
| | 29/11/18 | | 525 Company moved to CHAPOIS | M.T.S. |
| | 30/11/18 | | Too Large | M.T.S. |

J.M. [signature]
LIEUT. COLONEL
COMMDG. 62nd DIVISIONAL TRAIN

Confidential.

9824

# WAR DIARY.
## of the
### 62ND DIVISIONAL TRAIN.

From. 1.12.18.
To. 31.12.18.

## VOLUME. 24.

Original

R.S. Clayton
Major.
COMDG. 62ND DIVISIONAL TRAIN.

# WAR DIARY
## or
## INTELLIGENCE SUMMARY.

Army Form C. 2118.

(Erase heading not required.)

ORIGINAL

22ND DIVISIONAL TRAIN

| Place | Date | Hour | Summary of Events and Information | Remarks and references to Appendices |
|---|---|---|---|---|
| CORBION. | 1.12.18. | | Railhead OTHEE. Train Headquarters. CORBION. 525 Company GEMMECHENNE. 526 Company CHAPOIS. 527 Company CORBION. 528 Company ACHENE. | Initial |
| | 2.12.18. | | No change. | Initial |
| | 3.12.18. | | No change. | |
| | 4.12.18. | | No change. | |
| | 5.12.18. | | No change. | Initial |
| | 6.12.18. | | 526 Company moved to SOY. 185 Inf.Bde.Refilling point moved to SOY. | Initial |
| | 7.12.18. | | No change. | |
| | 8.12.18. | | No change. | |
| | 9.12.18. | | No change. | |
| | 10.12.18. | | 525 Company moved to CORBION. Refilling points. Div.troops moved to CORBION. 526 Company moved to CHARDENEU. 185 Inf.Bde. " to CHARDENEU. 527 Company moved to REMONT. 186 Inf.Bde. " to REMONT. 528 Company moved to MONTPLAISER. 187 Inf.Bde. " to MONTPLAISER. | Initial |
| | 11.12.18. | | Railhead ROUX. Refilling points. Div.troops moved to FALLON. T.H.Q. moved to FALLON. 185 Inf.Bde. " to VILLE. 525 Company moved to FALLON. 186 Inf.Bde. " to AMAS. 526 Company " to VILLE. 187 Inf.Bde. " to MONTPLAISER. 527 Company " to AMAS. 528 Company " to MONTPLAISER. | Initial |

Signed Major
Commanding 22nd DIVISIONAL TRAIN

# WAR DIARY or INTELLIGENCE SUMMARY.

*(Erase heading not required.)*

Army Form C. 2118.

**52ND DIVISIONAL TRAIN**  ORIGINAL

| Place | Date | Hour | Summary of Events and Information | Remarks and references to Appendices |
|---|---|---|---|---|
| HAMOIR. | 12.12.18. | | Railhead points. Div.Troops moved to OCQUIER. <br> 525 Company moved to NEUFY. <br> 526 Company " " to HOUPET. <br> 527 Company " " to NEBLON les XHOIGNES. <br> 528 Company " " to | |
| | 13.12.18. | | Railhead points. Div.Troops moved to VILLE. <br> 525 Company moved to GRAND HALLEUX. <br> 526 Company " " to CHAUVEHEID. <br> 527 Company " " to NEBLON. <br> 528 Company " " to HOUPET. | |
| VIELSALM. | 14.12.18. | | Railhead STAVELOT. <br> T.H.Q. moved to VIELSALM. <br> 525 Company moved to CHAUVEHEID. <br> 526 Company " " to VIELSALM. <br> 527 Company " " to HOURT. <br> 528 Company " " to HAUTE BODEUX. | |
| | 15.12.18. | | 187 Inf.Bde. Refilling point moved to BASSE BODEUX. | |
| | 16.12.18. | | Refilling points. Div.Troops moved to PARFONDRAY. <br> 525 Company moved to MIREELD. <br> 526 Company " " to FROKENSBORN. (Nr. ARUM) <br> 527 Company " " to <br> 528 Company " " to BASSE BODEUX. | |
| MALMEDY. | 17.12.18. | | Railhead BOURGLON. <br> T.H.Q. moved to MALMEDY. <br> 525 Company moved to WEISMES. <br> 526 Company " " to BULLINGEN. <br> 527 Company " " to MIREFLD. <br> 528 Company " " to MASTA. | |
| | 18.12.18. | | 187th Infantry Bde. Refilling point moved to WEISMES. | |
| | 19.12.18. | | No change. | |

H.Clayton
Major
a2 COMMAND 52nd DIVISIONAL TRAIN

Army Form C. 2118.

# WAR DIARY
## or
## INTELLIGENCE SUMMARY.
*(Erase heading not required.)*

ORIGINAL.

62ND DIVISION.

| Place | Date | Hour | Summary of Events and Information | Remarks and references to Appendices |
|---|---|---|---|---|
| MALMEDY. | 20.12.18. | | Railhead WEYWERTZ. | ntf |
| | 21.12.18. | | 528 Company moved to ELSENBORN CAMP. | ntf |
| | 22.12.18. | | 525 Company moved to LAGER ELSENBORN. <br> 526 Company " to MIESCHEID. <br> 528 Company " to ELSENBORN. | ntf |
| SCHLEIDEN. | 22.12.18. | | T.H.Q. moved to SCHLEIDEN. Refilling points. Div.troops moved to MONTJOIE. <br> 185 Inf.Bde. " to HELLENTHAL. <br> 186 Inf.Bde. " to NEUHAUS. <br> 187 Inf.Bde. " to HOFEN. | ntf |
| | 23.12.18. | | Refilling points. Div.troops moved to SCHLEIDEN. <br> 185 Inf.Bde. " to STRIMPT. <br> 186 Inf.Bde. " to HELLENTHAL. <br> 187 Inf.Bde. " to HERHAHN. | ntf |
| | 24.12.18. | | Refilling points. 185 Inf.Bde. moved to KOMMERN. <br> 186 Inf.Bde. " to DENKRATH. <br> 187 Inf.Bde. " to HERGARTEN. | ntf |
| | 25.12.18. | | Refilling points. Div.troops moved to OLEF. <br> 186 Inf.Bde. " to BREITEN BENDEN. <br> 187 Inf.Bde. " to WOLLERSHEIM. | ntf |
| | 26.12.18. | | 525 Company moved to SCHEVEN. Div.troops Refilling point moved to SCHEVEN. | ntf |
| | 27.12.18. | | No change. | |
| | 28.12.18. | | No change. | |

R.S.Clayton
Major
a/Commdr. 62nd Divisional Train.

Army Form C. 2118.

# WAR DIARY
## or
## INTELLIGENCE SUMMARY.

*(Erase heading not required.)*

62ND DIVISIONAL TRAIN.    ORIGINAL.

Summary of Events and Information

| Place | Date | Hour | | Remarks and references to Appendices |
|---|---|---|---|---|
| SCHLEIDEN. | 29.12.18. | | Railhead WEILERSWIST. | |
| | 30.12.18. | | Railhead LIGLERWIST. | |
| | 31.12.18. | | No change. | |

R S Clayton
Major
a/ COMMDR 62nd DIVISIONAL Train

Confidential

98 25

# WAR DIARY.
## of the
### 62ND DIVISIONAL TRAIN.

from 1.1.19
to 31.1.19

## VOLUME 25.

LIEUT. COLONEL,
COMMDG. 62ND DIVISIONAL TRAIN.

Original

**WAR DIARY**
*or*
**INTELLIGENCE SUMMARY**
(Erase heading not required.)

**62ND DIVISIONAL TRAIN**

Army Form C. 2118.

ORIGINAL

| Place | Date | Hour | Summary of Events and Information | Remarks and references to Appendices |
|---|---|---|---|---|
| SCHLEIDEN | 1.1.19 | | Railhead — MECHERNICH. | |
| | | | Train Headquarters SCHLEIDEN | |
| | | | 525 Company SCHEVEN | |
| | | | 526 Company KOMMERN | |
| | | | 527 Company BREITENBENDEN | |
| | | | 528 Company WOLLERSHEIM | |
| | | | 2/Lt Peirsman appointed for Rations. Repelling Panels Divisional Troops SCHEVEN | |
| | | | 183rd Brigade Supplies KOMMERN | |
| | | | 185th Brigade Supplies BREITENBENDEN | |
| | | | 187th Brigade Supplies WOLLERSHEIM | |
| | 2.1.19 | | No change | AJC |
| | 3.1.19 | | No change | AJC |
| | 4.1.19 | | No change | AJC |
| | 5.1.19 | | No change | AJC |
| | 6.1.19 | | No change | AJC |
| | 7.1.19 | | No change | AJC |
| | 8.1.19 | | No change | AJC |

H.H. Allen Bett
LIEUT. COLONEL
COMMDG. 62ND DIVISIONAL TRAIN

Army Form C. 2118.

ORIGINAL (2)

# WAR DIARY
## or
## INTELLIGENCE SUMMARY
(Erase heading not required.)

**82ND DIVISIONAL TRAIN**

Instructions regarding War Diaries and Intelligence Summaries are contained in F. S. Regs., Part II. and the Staff Manual respectively. Title pages will be prepared in manuscript.

| Place | Date | Hour | Summary of Events and Information | Remarks and references to Appendices |
|---|---|---|---|---|
| SCHLEIDEN | 9.1.19 | | 1 Reinforcement reported from Base | AHK |
| | 10.1.19 | | 1 Reinforcement reported from Base | AHK |
| | | | 1 Driver left for dispersal station | AHK |
| | 11.1.19 | | No change | AHK |
| | 12.1.19 | | No change | AHK |
| | 13.1.19 | | 6 O.Ranks left for dispersal stations | AHK |
| | 14.1.19 | | No change | AHK |
| | 15.1.19 | | No change | AHK |
| | 16.1.19 | | 5 Reinforcements reported from Base | AHK |
| | 17.1.19 | | No change | AHK |
| | 18.1.19 | | No change | AHK |
| | 19.1.19 | | 1 Reinforcement reported from Base | AHK |
| | 20.1.19 | | No change | AHK |
| | 21.1.19 | | No change | AHK |

A. M. Kuttner ?
LIEUT. COLONEL.
COMMDG. 82ND DIVISIONAL TRAIN

Army Form C. 2118.

# WAR DIARY

or

## INTELLIGENCE SUMMARY.

(Erase heading not required.)

**82ND DIVISIONAL TRAIN.**

ORIGINAL

Instructions regarding War Diaries and Intelligence Summaries are contained in F. S. Regs., Part II. and the Staff Manual respectively. Title pages will be prepared in manuscript.

| Place | Date | Hour | Summary of Events and Information | Remarks and references to Appendices |
|---|---|---|---|---|
| SCHEIDEN | 22.1.19 | | No change | |
| | 23.1.19 | | No change | |
| | 24.1.19 | | No change | |
| | 25.1.19 | | No change | |
| | 26.1.19 | | No change | |
| | 27.1.19 | | No change | |
| | 28.1.19 | | No change | |
| | 29.1.19 | | 1 Postal van left for Dispersal station | |
| | 30.1.19 | | 525 Company & Divisional Troops Refilling Point moved to OLEF | |
| | 31.1.19 | | No change | |

H. Wilson Pratt
LIEUT. COLONEL.
COMMDG. 82ND DIVISIONAL TRAIN.

Confidential

Original

WR 26

# WAR DIARY.
## of the
### 62ND DIVISIONAL TRAIN.

from 1.2.18.
to 28.2.18

## VOLUME 26.

LIEUT. COLONEL.
COMMDG. 62nd DIVISIONAL TRAIN.

Original

Army Form C. 2118.

# WAR DIARY
## or
## INTELLIGENCE SUMMARY.

(Erase heading not required.)

Instructions regarding War Diaries and Intelligence Summaries are contained in F. S. Regs., Part II. and the Staff Manual respectively. Title pages will be prepared in manuscript.

## 62nd DIVISIONAL TRAIN.

| Place | Date | Hour | Summary of Events and Information | Remarks and references to Appendices |
|---|---|---|---|---|
| SCHLEIDEN | 1.2.19 | | Position NECHERNICH | |
| | | | Hon. Headquarters  SCHLEIDEN | |
| | | | 525 Company  OLEF | |
| | | | 526 Company  KOMMERN | |
| | | | 527 Company  BREITEN BENDEN | |
| | | | 528 Company  WOLLERSHEIM | |
| | 2.2.19 | | No change | |
| | 3.2.19 | | No change | |
| | 4.2.19 | | No change | |
| | 5.2.19 | | 5 Men ex. 4.15 Concentration Camp. DUREN. | |
| | 6.2.19 | | 1 L/D Meule & 9 NC.Men transferred from Field Ambulances to Train | |
| | | | 1 Man sent to Concentration Camp DUREN. | |
| | 7.2.19 | | No change | |
| | 8.2.19 | | 2 Lieut Grayson died whilst on leave in England | |
| | 9.2.19 | | No change | |

Rgstling  Divn. Bil. Offr.  OLEF
185 Brigade Group  KOMMERN
186 Brigade Group  BREITEN BENDEN
187 Brigade Group  WOLLERSHEIM

LIEUT. COLONEL
COMMDG. 62ND DIVISIONAL TRAIN.

Original.

Army Form C. 2118.

# WAR DIARY
## or
## INTELLIGENCE SUMMARY.

(Erase heading not required.)

Instructions regarding War Diaries and Intelligence
Summaries are contained in F. S. Regs., Part II.
and the Staff Manual respectively. Title pages
will be prepared in manuscript.

| Place | Date | Hour | Summary of Events and Information | Remarks and references to Appendices |
|---|---|---|---|---|
| | | | 82ND DIVISIONAL TRAIN. | |
| SCHLEIDEN | 10.2.19 | | No change | |
| | 11.2.19 | | No change | |
| | 12.2.19 | | 5 men sent to Concentration Camp DUREN. | |
| | 13.2.19 | | No change | |
| | 14.2.19 | | 1 man sent to Concentration Camp DUREN | |
| | 15.2.19 | | No change | |
| | 16.2.19 | | No change | |
| | 17.2.19 | | No change. Temperatures rising | |
| | 18.2.19 | | Divisional Troops supplies sent by rail to BEYOND embarquéd from here | |
| | 19.2.19 | | 1 reinforcement received from base | |
| | | | 1 man sent to Concentration Camp DUREN. | |
| | 20.2.19 | | No change | |
| | 21.2.19 | | 3 men sent to Concentration Camp DUREN. | |
| | 22.2.19 | | No change | |
| | 23.2.19 | | No change | |

W.H. Gallagher
LIEUT. OC ONE?
COMMDG. 82ND DIVISIONAL TRAIN.

Army Form C. 2118.

Original.

# WAR DIARY
## or
## INTELLIGENCE SUMMARY.
(Erase heading not required.)

62ND DIVISIONAL TRAIN

| Place | Date | Hour | Summary of Events and Information | Remarks and references to Appendices |
|---|---|---|---|---|
| SCHLEIDEN | 24.2.19 | | No change | |
| | 25.2.19 | | No change. Normal conditions for traffic resumed on & after 27/2/16 | |
| | 26.2.19 | | No change | |
| | 27.2.19 | | 3 reinforcement drivers rec'd from 10th Division | |
| | 28.2.19 | | No change. | |

H H Wilkinson
LIEUT. COL. OMDG
COMMDG. 62ND DIVISIONAL TRAIN

CONFIDENTIAL. ORIGINAL.

Vol I

H.Q. HIGHLAND
DIVL. TRAIN.
R.A.S.C.
No. 72/727
Date

# WAR DIARY

OF

## HIGHLAND DIVISIONAL TRAIN.

From: 1st March 1919.
To: 31st March 1919.

Volume: 26.

A Witherspoon Lyle Hay
LIEUT.-COLONEL,
COMMDG HIGHLAND DIVISIONAL TRAIN.

Army Form C. 2118.

# WAR DIARY
## or
## INTELLIGENCE SUMMARY.
(Erase heading not required.)

Instructions regarding War Diaries and Intelligence Summaries are contained in F. S. Regs., Part II. and the Staff Manual respectively. Title pages will be prepared in manuscript.

## HIGHLAND DIVISIONAL TRAIN   Summary of Events and Information

| Place | Date | Hour | Summary of Events and Information | Remarks and references to Appendices |
|---|---|---|---|---|
| SCHLEIDEN | 1.3.19 | | Routined MECHERNICH | |
| | | | Base. H.Q. SCHLEIDEN | |
| | | | 525 Company & Divisional Baths Refilling Point OLEF | |
| | | | 526 Company & 125 Bde Gp. KOMMERN R.P. | |
| | | | 527 Company & 126 Bde Gp. BREITENBENDEN R.P. | |
| | | | 528 Company & 127 Bde Gp. WOLLERSHEIM R.P. | |
| | 2.3.19 | | No change | |
| | 3.3.19 | | No change | |
| | 4.3.19 | | No change | |
| | 5.3.19 | | No change | |
| | 6.3.19 | | 528 Company & 127 Bde RP moved to DUREN | |
| | 7.3.19 | | 187 Brigade reached DUREN | |
| | 8.3.19 | | No change | |
| | 9.3.19 | | No change | |
| | 10.3.19 | | No change | |

LIEUT. COLONEL,
COMMDG HIGHLAND DIVISIONAL TRAIN.

Army Form C. 2118.

# WAR DIARY
## or
## INTELLIGENCE SUMMARY.
(Erase heading not required.)

Instructions regarding War Diaries and Intelligence Summaries are contained in F. S. Regs., Part II. and the Staff Manual respectively. Title pages will be prepared in manuscript.

HIGHLAND DIVISIONAL TRAIN  Summary of Events and Information

| Place | Date | Hour | Summary of Events and Information | Remarks and references to Appendices |
|---|---|---|---|---|
| SCHLEIDEN | 11.3.19 | | 527 Company & 134 Brigade R.T. moved to OLLESHEIM | |
| | 12.3.19 | | No change | |
| | 13.3.19 | | Gen. Headquarters moved to DUREN | |
| | 14.3.19 | | 528 Company and 115 Brigade R.T. moved to FROITZHEIM | |
| | 15.3.19 | | 136 Brigade moved to DUREN | |
| | 16.3.19 | | 528 Company & 137 Brigade R.T. moved to DISTELRATH. 529 Company & 153 Brigade R.T. moved to MERZEN | |
| | | | Lieut. Stewart A.R.T.M.H.D.T. O.S.B. assumes command of the Train | am |
| | 17.3.19 | | No change | |
| | 18.3.19 | | No change | |
| | 19.3.19 | | No change | |
| | 20.3.19 | | No change | |
| | 21.3.19 | | No change | |
| | 22.3.19 | | No change | |
| | 23.3.19 | | No change | |
| | 24.3.19 | | No change | |

A.V.  
LIEUT. COLONEL  
COMMDG HIGHLAND DIVISIONAL TRAIN.

Army Form C. 2118.

# WAR DIARY
## or
## INTELLIGENCE SUMMARY.
*(Erase heading not required.)*

Instructions regarding War Diaries and Intelligence Summaries are contained in F. S. Regs., Part II. and the Staff Manual respectively. Title pages will be prepared in manuscript.

HIGHLAND DIVISIONAL TRAIN  Summary of Events and Information

| Place | Date | Hour | | Remarks and references to Appendices |
|---|---|---|---|---|
| DUREN | 25.3.19 | | No change | |
| | 26.3.19 | | No change | |
| | 27.3.19 | | No change | |
| | 28.3.19 | | No change | |
| | 29.3.19 | | No change | |
| | 30.3.19 | | No change | |
| | 31.3.19 | | No change | |

A. R. Purcell
LIEUT. COLONEL
COMMDG HIGHLAND DIVISIONAL TRAIN.

Army Form C. 2118.

526-8

DUPLICATE

WOOLWICH DOCKYARD
A.S.C. RECORDS
9 MAY 1919

# WAR DIARY
or
## INTELLIGENCE SUMMARY
(Erase heading not required.)

## HIGHLAND DIVISIONAL TRAIN Summary of Events and Information

| Place | Date | Hour | Summary of Events and Information | Remarks |
|---|---|---|---|---|
| DUREN | 1-4-19 | | Received MECHERNICH for Lieut Hughes & 183 Brigade & DUREN for 186 & 187 Brigades. | |
| | | | From HQ DUREN | |
| | | | 526 Company & Lieut Hughes resting point OLEF. | |
| | | | 526   "   & 185 Brigade   "    "   FROITZHEIM | |
| | | | 527   "   & 186   "    "    "   KERPEN | |
| | | | 528   "   & 187   "    "    "   DISTELRATH | |
| | 2-4-19 | | 2nd Lieut W.S. Clarke reported his arrival from the 20th W.Dis. Coy and posted to 527 Company as Supply Officer vice 2nd Lt A.J. Young. | |
| | 3-4-19 | | 2/Lieut C.M. Le Grice reported his arrival from the 21 H.Dis. Bn and posted to 525 Company as Supply Officer vice 2/Lieut E.A. Wagner. | |
| | 4-4-19 | | Exchange. | |
| | 5-4-19 | | 2/Lieut C.S. Garner reported his arrival from the 25th H.Divisional Train and posted to 525 Company. | |
| | | | 2/Lieut M.A. Chalziger reported his arrival from the 25th H.Divisional Train posted to 526 Company. | |

Army Form C. 2118.

# WAR DIARY
## or
## INTELLIGENCE SUMMARY
(Erase heading not required.)

HIGHLAND DIVISIONAL TRAIN Summary of Events and Information

| Place | Date | Hour | Summary of Events and Information | Remarks and references to Appendices |
|---|---|---|---|---|
| DÜREN | 5.4.19 | | 1/Sent L.C. Wall reported hisarrival from the 20th Divisional Train | |
| | | | Posted to 528 Company | |
| | 6.4.19 | | 1/Sent S. Brearshead Watright on Draft 11 "Lanns" transferred eight to France for 3 months Eye Medical Board. No change | |
| | 7.4.19 | | 527 Company and 186 Bequests of thing front moved to BIRGEL. Lieut G. A. Hare O.C. King Company of the 20th Div. Train as an All Wagon | |
| | 7.4.19. | | 1/Cpl L.R. Lloyd The bistrar covered to the 21st Reserve Horse Depot | |
| | 9.4.19 | | 1/2 2 Company | |
| | | | 1/Cpl E. M. Morris RASC who has covered to and for the 30th Battery RFA | |
| | | | No. 4 Company | |
| | | | Private E. M. Lane who has covered to and from How Horse Depot rejoins | |
| | | | Pte G. Pendenham Pte 1 Company | |
| | | | Rejoining from Leeds after 6 months annual from the 13th Bn & Loan rejoined his unit | |
| | | | No. 3 Company | |
| | | | 1/Sergt J. Hurd after attending course at How Horse Depot returned to Company | |
| | | | Posted to 527 Company and attached to R. J. Company | |

Army Form C. 2118.

# WAR DIARY
## or
## INTELLIGENCE SUMMARY.
*(Erase heading not required.)*

DUPLICATE

Instructions regarding War Diaries and Intelligence Summaries are contained in F. S. Regs., Part II. and the Staff Manual respectively. Title pages will be prepared in manuscript.

## HIGHLAND DIVISIONAL TRAIN Summary of Events and Information

| Place | Date | Hour | Summary of Events and Information | Remarks and references to Appendices |
|---|---|---|---|---|
| DUREN | 10.4.19 | | No change | |
| | 11.4.19 | | No change | |
| | 12.4.19 | | No change | |
| | 13.4.19 | | 2/Lieut. C. Bryant transferred to "D" Supremal Train and rest of personnel of the Highland Divisional Train. | |
| | | | 2/Lieut. F.W. Hopkins to "D" Supremal Train taken on the strength of the Highland Divisional Train. | |
| | | | 2/Lieut. J.B. Tylden "D" Supremal Train taken on the strength of the Highland Divisional Train. | |
| | 14.4.19 | | No change. | |
| | 15.4.19 | | 2/Lieut Wm. P. Purcell to return to the U.K. for Demobilisation and is struck off the strength of the Train from 75 instant. | |
| | 16.4.19 | | No change | |
| | 17.4.19 | | No change | |
| | 18.4.19 | | 2/Lieut. A. Byrd offered today to Artley's Board at Lines H.S.H.A.F.G. was found to be temporarily unfit for general service. In no event of his being again fit for Sickness for General Service, he should be re-boarded as he cannot at the present moment be spared from employment to perform the duties of his Command. | |

D. D. & L., London, E.C.

(A 10260) Wt W5300/P713 750,000 2/15 Sch. 83 Forms/C2118/16

Army Form C. 2118.

# WAR DIARY
## or
## INTELLIGENCE SUMMARY
*(Erase heading not required.)*

DUPLICATE

**HIGHLAND DIVISIONAL TRAIN** Summary of Events and Information

| Place | Date | Hour | Summary of Events and Information | Remarks and references to Appendices |
|---|---|---|---|---|
| DUREN | 19-4-19 | | 7/Highland Field Amb joined the 39th Highland Div Amb and vacated by the H.T. 378/Coy on the 18th. 6/7th Highland Divisional Train now this establishment. | |
| | | | Lieut R Gordon M.C. took over duties and vacated Capt W.H. Gray R.A.S.C. | |
| | | | Capt H.A. Buchanan this unit and Capt W.H. Gray R.A.S.C | |
| | 20-4-19 | | Hqrs Div arrived from 3rd Div Train and was posted to 528 Company RASC | |
| | 21-4-19 | | No change. | |
| | 22-4-19 | | No change. | |
| | 23-4-19 | | Capt John Whitley took over command of 528 Coy RASC from Capt C.H. Hare | |
| | 24-4-19 | | No change. (S.S.O.) left for demobilization and was struck off strength. Capt C.H. Hare returned to duties of S.S.O. 7Capt P.H. Chance assigned Lieut of Hospital after being incap. from Capt A.K. Kitson. Immed option of Lieut's return to this | |
| | 25-4-19 | | Guards Division orders being drawn in RASC, 12 hr. Lt(Capt) E Boolan joined from Guards Div. Train, and was taken in strength. | |
| | 26-4-19 | | C.O. visited 527 Coy in morning. Lt(Capt) Boolan taken to that Company. Visit to 526 Coy in afternoon. H.T. drew from Duren railhead 8.30am for 2/ Highland Bde and 1st Line Supplies drawn from Refilling Pt. to Q.M. Stores. Manoeuvre. Lt/Capt E. Boolan took on command of 527 Coy from Lt Capt S.H. Hutchinson. | |
| | 27-4-19 | | kit HQ. moved to KREUZAU. Brit Train and MT Coy remained in DUREN. MT drew from Railhead DUREN for DA group. MECHERNICH closed as their railhead. | |
| | 28-4-19 | | No change. | |
| | 29-4-19 | | C.O. visited Add Coy at OLEF. | |
| | 30-4-19 | | | |

A.R.Russell
LIEUT. COLONEL,
COMMDG HIGHLAND DIVISIONAL TRAIN.

Confidential

War Diary

of

Highland Divisional Train

From 1st May 1919 to 31st May 1919

Army Form C. 2118.

# WAR DIARY
## or
## INTELLIGENCE SUMMARY.
*(Erase heading not required.)*

H.Q. HIGHLAND. DIVL. TRAIN

MAY 1919

Instructions regarding War Diaries and Intelligence Summaries are contained in F. S. Regs., Part II. and the Staff Manual respectively. Title pages will be prepared in manuscript.

| Place | Date | Hour | Summary of Events and Information | Remarks and references to Appendices |
|---|---|---|---|---|
| DUREN. | 1-5-19 | | ~~Absorption was today~~ T/Major F.B. HARDY having reported his arrival from MIDLAND DIV¹ TRAIN is taken on the strength from to-day's date, and is posted to No1 Coy. | |
| | 2-5-19 | | Capt. C.H. MASSÉ proceeded on leave to U.K. Leave to date from 3-5-19 to 17-5-19. Remains in normal | |
| | | | Capt. F.H. HUTCHINS. R.A.S.C. (S.R.) proceeded to England prior to joining the EGYPTIAN E. Force and is struck off the strength of the unit from to day's date | |
| | | | 9/Capt. G.S. SHAW-RIGBY (T.F) proceeded on leave (14 days) to U.K | |
| | 3.5.19 | | Remains in normal | |
| | 4.5.19 | | Remains in normal | |
| | 5.5.19 | | Remains in normal o/c Train accompanied by A.A. toured Highland Division pack mule to Hqrs 2, 3, 1-4 Coys of the Train. | |
| | 6.5.19 | | No change | |
| | 7.5.19 | | No1 Coy of the Train moved to HERGARTEN by march route from OIEF – Refilling Point HERGARTEN Villages | |
| | 8.5.19 | | No change | |
| | 9.5.19 | | Remains in normal | |
| | 10.5.19 | | Remains in normal | |
| | 11.5.19 | | " " " | |
| | 12.5.19 | | " " " | |
| | 13.5.19 | | " " " | |
| | 14.5.19 | | " " " | |
| | 15.5.19 | | | |

Army Form C. 2118.

# WAR DIARY
## or
## INTELLIGENCE SUMMARY.
(Erase heading not required.)

Instructions regarding War Diaries and Intelligence Summaries are contained in F. S. Regs., Part II. and the Staff Manual respectively. Title pages will be prepared in manuscript.

H.Q. Highland Divl Train

Month: May 1919

| Place | Date | Hour | Summary of Events and Information | Remarks and references to Appendices |
|---|---|---|---|---|
| DUREN | 16.5.19 | | Routine in camp | |
| | 17.5.19 | | Capt. W.M. WHITTY RASC. proceeded on leave to U.K. (18 May – 1 June) | |
| | 18.5.19 | | Coy/Adjt. C.H. MACSE returned from leave. Capt S.G. Shaw returned from leave | |
| | 19.5.19 | | Infantrymen to Tempe & RASC reported to Base Coys. | |
| | 20.5.19 | | Lt Col. A.R. LIDDELL proceeded on leave to U.K. Major F.B. HARDY assumed temporary command of Highland Divl Train. G.O.C. bid L/Col A.R. LIDDELL farewell on his road to KREUZAU 5 km off (D.C. Train present. Staff Officers invited) | |
| | 21.5.19 | | G.O.C. held conference at 6pm at very short notice. Major HARDY, ADJT and S.S.O. present. Verbal warning of hostile advance across RHINE via DA OEG 23-4. Coys warned to be ready to move at a moments notice via Pam-22Y | |
| | 22.5.19 | | 1st and 2nd Recc. asked to supply weapons in emergency. Mr J.A. STEVEN proceeded on conducted/baft leave Party. V.C.C. LIDDELL returned from BOULOGNE in afternoon & warmly welcomed | |
| | 23.5.19 | 21:45 | Received 21:45 hrs followed by further addenda. Further details of tactical train transport and amendments to existing war arrangement by one Entraining Strength required by Camp Commandant. Further details of scheme for move. Otherwise no change | |
| | 24.5.19 | | No change. Usual routine. Capt J.A. Sykes proceeded on leave 26.5.19 – 9.6.19 | |
| | 25.5.19 | | Reorganizing officers and subalterns began scheme for opening training amongst transport team 27.5.19 D.A. new arr. methods in cases of one Company Commanders drill in ward area while relieve and administrative duties | |
| | 26.5.19 | | | |
| | 27.5.19 | | | |
| | 28.5.19 | | No change. Usual routine. Confts from Q.M.N.G. arrived to Bde H.Qrs.–H.Qrs. | |
| | 29.5.19 | | D.A. turning over farewell. H.D. bearing order No 8 received 19.30 Slight changes | |
| | 30.5.19 | | No change | |
| | 31.5.19 | | Staff Lieuts attending wheeled 1st Bde area, including 51 bty R.A.SC. Col. Roy, Chief Inspector Q.M.G. Scottish Command Highland Divl Train area 1000 hr. | |

A.R. Russell
LIEUT. COLONEL
COMMDG HIGHLAND DIVISIONAL TRAIN.

Army Form C. 2118.

# WAR DIARY
## or
## INTELLIGENCE SUMMARY.
(Erase heading not required.)

H.Q. Highland Armoured ......

June 1919.

| Place | Date | Hour | Summary of Events and Information | Remarks and references to Appendices |
|---|---|---|---|---|
| DÜREN | 1-6-19 | | Usual routine. No change. | C/tts |
| | 2-6-19 | | Capt. E.C. Linnen proceeded on leave to U.K. 2/6 – 16/6/19. Capt. Holm White returned from leave. Usual routine. | C/tts |
| | 3-6-19 | | Cpl. Wm. White attached to 1st Canadian Sqn. to reconstitute S.S.O. C.M.G. in H.Q. Brigade Armoured 3.6.19. Usual routine. Capt. E.St. Hurst awarded M.C. in Gazette 3/3/19. | C/tts |
| | 4-6-19 | | Usual routine. No change. | C/tts |
| | 5-6-19 6-6-19 | | Sgt. Wheatley and Sgt. Fenbury awarded M.S.M. in Gazette 4/4/19. No change. Usual routine. Plating repaired on U.K. tonnes heavy lorry 2/6/19. Board of officers on S.I.S. Corps vehicles indent deficiencies. Some difficulty was returned to the units on account of bad contact-breakers. Returned to RASC and refractedly returned rifles and of 74 West Riding Field Ambulance absorbed into Reinf. | C/tts |
| | 7-6-19 | | Lt. J.A. Stevens returned from leave. 7/6. Lt J.L. Thomas reported no arrival from 13th Cavalry Bde. R.A.S.C. and is taken on strength from today. State medical history sheets or in envelopes accompanying. | C/tts |
| | 8-6-19 | | No change. | C/tts |
| | 9-6-19 | | Lt. A.P. Guest proceeded on leave to U.K. 10-6-19 to 24-6-19. and returned by 4th I.S.A. Open Transport. | C/tts |
| | 10-6-19 | | Capt. E.A. Sykes returned from leave. Ordinary routine. Lt. T. Hinge reported his arrival from 2nd Artillery Command Carpenters Section & Dupnent loader on duty and has been took accounts and carrying out his duty to M2ky. | C/tts |
| | 11-6-19 | | Lt. KY Berge taken on strength from today. | C/tts |
| | 12-6-19 | | Capt. P.M. Chance proceeded on leave 13-6-19 – 27-6-19 to U.K. Capt. Van Elliott acting for him. | C/tts |
| | 13-6-19 | | Usual routine. D.A. Mure in case of absence assumed. Usual routine. | C/tts |
| | 14-6-19 | | Lt. Colo. E. Sim proceeded on leave to U.K. from 15-6-19 – 29-10-19. Lt. Hurll and Lt. Ritman 627 M.C. Bn attended preliminary findings and were attached to Highland Bde. Train for the above interview. | C/tts |

# WAR DIARY
## or
## INTELLIGENCE SUMMARY.

(Erase heading not required.) Page (2)

Army Form C. 2118.

Head Quarters Highland Divisional Train

June 1919

| Place | Date | Hour | Summary of Events and Information | Remarks and references to Appendices |
|---|---|---|---|---|
| DÜREN. | 15-6-19 | | 2/Lt Hall and 2/Lt Reid were attached to 525 Coy and 528 Coy respectively. Highland Divisional G.915 and 916. Urgent warning of purchase dated 17 July. Camps warned of purchase dates of 17 July, in evening. | e/c |
| | | p.m. | | |
| | 16-6-19 | | Wisdom No. G.929 received. | e/c |
| | 17-6-19 | 14.55h | G.953 received. Today 20th June. Today is 3rd day for the transport group head to MUNGERSDORF. Officers on leave recalled, then were cancelled by C.O. permission. Camp Coms. misled Divs Coms are drilling. 528 Coy and 3rd Pk. group transport hired by road to MUNGERSDORF. Pts group marched to OPLADEN. No. 2. To DA warning No.(3) received. C.O. went forward to see the new area. Amendment — | e/c |
| | 18-6-19 | | 527 Coy formed to SOLINGEN. 528 Coy continued march to OPLADEN. 526 Coy first stage FROITZHEIM to MUNGERSDORF. 9 day railhead no 48hr interval was given for | e/c |
| | 19-6-19 | | | |
| | 20-6-19 | | S.S.O. (Capt which T.) went forward to Liet at OHLIGS with forward Route Times to 3 Advanced Supply Depots. Have been informed and the Road west than Ex. DA group arrived locating not were fed partly from DÜREN and partly from OHLIGS a 48 mile lorry trip. Adjutant march 527 Coy in SOLINGEN. As well there 528 Coy established in HILDEN having arrived 526 Coy continued march to OPLADEN. | e/c |
| | 21-6-19 | | after arrival. Left behind to feeding Dump. Small parties destitute of of feeding transport in attacking arm to DA groups. They field station were returned to town in road and then forwarded at other advanced feeding stations. | e/c |
| | 22-6-19 | | by lorry to town. Hunt W.S. Roberts returned from leave. | e/c |
| | 23-6-19 | | Their Relation Indirectly take us parties of S.O. Div Artillery group from tent at Bavou. H.T. Lee houses material lion out of 16th Army Auxiliary H.T. Coy at MÜLHEIM: Greenspan reported. Ammunition DA group from Rio DÜREN. | e/c |

Army Form C. 2118.

# WAR DIARY
## or
## INTELLIGENCE SUMMARY.
(Erase heading not required.) Page 3

Headquarters
Highland Division Train

Instructions regarding War Diaries and Intelligence Summaries are contained in F. S. Regs., Part II. and the Staff Manual respectively. Title pages will be prepared in manuscript.

| Place | Date | Hour | Summary of Events and Information | Remarks and references to Appendices |
|---|---|---|---|---|
| DUREN | 24-6-19 | | Capt. E.C. Lunn took over duties as S.O. 1st Bde. from Lt. Stearn. Leave re-opened. | |
| " | 25-6-19 | | Administrative Instructions to return of 3 A.S.C. F.DUREN were received. Highland Division Order No. 9 received. Also S.S.O.'s orders to S.En. Capt. F.S. Sykes assumed Temporary command of 528 Coy. Lieut. A.P. Ewart returned from leave. | |
| " | 26-6-19 | | | |
| " | 27-6-19 | | Capt. Clutz came to talk over orders + car of return move. | |
| " | 28-6-19 | | Lt. S. Hunter proceeded for detached duty. Capt. Clause returned from leave. Peace signed in afternoon. Notification of A'day being 30th received by wire also. | from 28-6-19 inclusive no demonstration |
| " | 29-6-19 | | Reconnaissance to newdeis to supplement to June 3rd Begat's proceeded to Division A. Sept. sch. W.O.T. to O.T.E. and 1/Capt. P.M. Chance + P.S. Handy O.T.E. Lt-Col A.R. Little proceeded on leave 30-6-19 to 14-7-19 and 7 mays for subsistence allowance in lieu of rations for 21-6-19. Lt. C. Lo. to Ewen returned from leave. Capt. (1/Capt) R Bordoli proceeded on leave 1-7-19 to 15-7-19. Lieut. F.R. Noyes assumed command of 527 Coy. 'A' day, 1st Highland Rda. moved to DUREN area; 1st Div transport under charge of 528 Coy stayed at MUNGERSDORF. | |

M.B. Hardy Major RASC
for LIEUT. COLONEL
COMMDG HIGHLAND DIVISIONAL TRAIN

# WAR DIARY

**Army Form C. 2118.**

Place: **HQ Highland Divisional Train**
Month and Year: **July 1919**

| Place | Date | Hour | Summary of Events and Information | Remarks and references to Appendices |
|---|---|---|---|---|
| DÜREN. | 1-7-19 | | 526 Coy arrived at FROITZHEIM. 528 Coy marched from HILDEN to OPLADEN. Received cloud address. | Cash |
| | 2-7-19 | | 526 Coy marched from OPLADEN to MÜNGERSDORF. 527 Coy marched from SOLINGEN to OPLADEN. 7/Capt. R.H. Chance u-assumed duties of S.S.O. from Capt. With Utility who returned attached to Train HQ. Railway normal again at DÜREN. | Cash |
| | 3-7-19 | | 528 Coy reported in from W Capt. Utility as escorting. 527 Coy marched to MÜNGERSDORF. Capt. Sid Utility as assumed command of 528 Coy from Capt Sykes. | Cash |
| | 4-7-19 | | 528 Coy [illeg] visiting [illeg] through Paris 9 miles exchanged of 9LD with HQ 310 and 311 Brens Res Signal Section. 527 Coy marched to L BURGEL. Lt Grist returned ex BURGEL. | Cash |
| | 5-7-19 | | 7/Lt M.T. Taylor reported his arrival from 12th A.A.H.T Coy and is [illeg] Visiting [illeg] in Paris. Crew received clue detail from Cargo dale Train. [illeg] L Coy. [illeg] detail. | Cash |
| | 6-7-19 | | Visitor heart [illeg] inserted and first [illeg] when [illeg] detail 10.30 a.m. from DÜREN. Capt Kerr [illeg] [illeg] with 1 officer and 6 other ranks and 10 OR for Company. | Cash |
| | 7-7-19 | | Perm visiting [illeg] hearty emptied and left DÜREN for COLOGNE 10.56. [illeg] taph an command of 526. 10 horses of Brit Signal Coy effects White [illeg] Brit with Companies and across Park of 6 Rainland. Coy from Capt Shaw. | Cash |
| | 8-7-19 | | Contract holiday. No particulars [illeg] to sports above but 525 Coy had arm. Rugby Kept Shaw proceeded f disposal and was struck off strength of Highland Rail Train. did not [illeg]. | Cash |
| | 9-7-19 | | S.O.E. conference 10.30 hrs. 4/O and SSO. present. question of Training, [illeg] Travel of men, demobilization, amalgamation of divisions discipline discussed. [illeg] [illeg] presented for different and in which of strength of Highland Divisional Train. Wks IO Today abroad in [illeg]. | Cash |

Army Form C. 2118.

Head Quarters.
Highland Divisional Train

# WAR DIARY
or
## INTELLIGENCE SUMMARY.
(Erase heading not required.) (Page 2)

Instructions regarding War Diaries and Intelligence Summaries are contained in F.S. Regs., Part II. and the Staff Manual respectively. Title pages will be prepared in manuscript.

| Place | Date | Hour | Summary of Events and Information | Remarks and references to Appendices |
|---|---|---|---|---|
| DÜREN. | 10-7-19 | | ⅔Capt. C.E. Lanan proceeded to Cologne and is struck off strength of Highland Divisional Train. AD.M.G. IV Corps acquainted S.S.O. to No1 Coy relieving him. | C.W.W. |
| | 11-7-19 | | Ordinary routine. No change. | C.W.W. |
| | 12-7-19 | | Information received verbally from Record Station G.H.Q. about 1945 Infantry transfers being affected. Held A.C. List return from hand. hand routine. | C.W.W. |
| | 13-7-19 | | Hot [crossed out] 2.3.4th Coys [crossed out] No change hand routine | C.W.W. |
| | 14-7-19 | | hand routine. Details of his own clarifiers received and Conference arranged | C.W.W. |
| | 15-7-19 | | Hot Train visited 2.3.4 Coys. Examined books, supplies etc. | C.W.W. |
| | 16-7-19 | | hand routine. No change. "Capt. E. Borden returned from leave. | C.W.W. |
| | 17-7-19 | | Enquiries made at G.H.Q. regarding civilian additions. Paris victory march party returned in evening. | C.W.W. |
| | 18-7-19 | | hand routine. No change. | C.W.W. |
| | 19-7-19 | | Peace celebration holiday throughout the Train. | C.W.W. |
| | 20-7-19 | | Hot Train visited 2nd and 3rd Coys. D.O.M. seen about horses. Held A.C. List with one No change. | C.W.W. |
| | 21-7-19 | | hand routine | C.W.W. |

# WAR DIARY
## or
## INTELLIGENCE SUMMARY
(Erase heading not required.) (Page 3)

Army Form C. 2118.

Headquarters Highland Divisional Train

| Place | Date | Hour | Summary of Events and Information | Remarks and references to Appendices |
|---|---|---|---|---|
| DÜREN | 22-7-19 | | Lt Col Addcaul returned from leave in U.K. | CWb |
| | 23-7-19 | | C.O. went to G.H.Q. about 1914-15 personnel, officers, leaves & OS.6 Corps re Pay and horse Book system coming into effect 1-8-19. T. BEATSON, 3rd Serjeants referred for Company duty with Highland Divisional Train. | CWb |
| | 24-7-19 | | 7/1/Lt T. Beatson, 3rd Serjeants attached to 525 Coy RASC for Company duty and instruction. C.O. visited Brig and IV Corps HQ area Commandant re area about DISTELRATH area and bad sanitation. | CWb |
| | 25-7-19 | | C.O. visited 526-525-527-528 Coys in order to select best G.S. wagon and complete team out of Brig Horse Show Event :- 525 began, 527 horses and harness, wheelers; 528 best H.D. stripped. 525 best L.D. stripped. | CWb |
| | | | 7/Lieut A.W. TAYLOR posted to Highland Divisional Train from 210 Coy (A.H.T.) ROUEN and taken on the strength. | |
| | 26-7-19 | | Visited A.W. TAYLOR posted to 525 Coy to complete company establishment. In charge stores. | GWb |
| | 27-7-19 | | Horses for Brig Horse Show proceeded to 525 Coy as being nearest to show ground. A.D.S.T. (P) Lt Col Co. MARKS called in afternoon. IV Corps Commander garden party Co attended. | CWb |
| | 28-7-19 | | C.O. went to G.H.Q. about leaves from infantry. British War medal ribbon issued to personnel at T.H.Q. | CWb |
| | 29-7-19 | | Brig Horse Show near HEIMBACH. Highland Div Train won lost 1st in Col C.N. horses and first A.P. Brig. Should change and extend to 5 horses military competition | CWb |

Army Form C. 2118.

# WAR DIARY
## or
## INTELLIGENCE SUMMARY.

(Erase heading not required.)

Headquarters
Highland Divisional Train

| Place | Date | Hour | Summary of Events and Information | Remarks and references to Appendices |
|---|---|---|---|---|
| DÜREN | 30-7-19 | | No change. List of 1914-15 retained soldiers forwarded EDHQ A. | Cook |
| | 31-7-19 | 12.00 | Rhine Army Horse Show meeting at G office 11.15 hrs. Eliminating show arranged to take place this hr and G. Lieut T. Taylor ordered to act from 6-8-19. All Leave cancelled by A/L 76. T/Lt Lt MEAD reported his arrival from 16th AHT Coy and is taken on the strength of Highland Divl Train. Posted to train HQ and attached E.S.O. 1st Bde for instruction in supply work. | Ellen |

A.Russell
LIEUT. COLONEL,
COMMDG HIGHLAND DIVISIONAL TRAIN.

Confidential.

War Diary
of
Highland Divisional Train.

From August 1st 1919   to August 12th 1919.

# WAR DIARY or INTELLIGENCE SUMMARY

Army Form C. 2118.

Head Quarters Highland Division

August 1919

| Place | Date | Hour | Summary of Events and Information | Remarks and references to Appendices |
|---|---|---|---|---|
| DUREN | 1-8-19 | | Usual routine. Col Liddell called in at GHQ in afternoon. | |
| | 2-8-19 | | Lt Liddell visited Highland BN (?) Heard the division was complete to proceed to England. No change. It says returning from leave (?) UK etc being wasted, leave under 7 days so is cancelled. | |
| | 3-8-19 | | No change, and no details of him to UK. | |
| | 4-8-19 | | Col Liddell went to DDMS. Forecast of arrangements for men received. | |
| | 5-8-19 | | SSO and Adjutant went to see AA & QMG. Further demand administration was received. 800 horses to replace HBS in supply units. A new unit L. Corp. Paigge-wagon (broken) and harness now to write. Outlining strength, Officers not ORs asked for. Outline of defence antipers of 1914-1915. | |
| | 6-8-19 | | Rates of personnel and equipment. Train received and Exp. wanted. They wanted to have L. Duren in B2 on all main lines to P1 in g/s and there are other vehicles to have vehicles from HERAARTEN return. | |
| | 7-8-19 | | 3 Cops ashen and equipment parked in PARADE STRASSE and kit taken to station. | |
| | 8-8-19 | | All known 1 Brig. train collected at D Coy Ammn. Collecting Camp ready to proceed to COLOGNE (24 Vety HP) Capt FH Sykes NTO Leyla I/c an 800 to set No 1 Coy walked from old area L DUREN, deleted in transit and equipment also packed close from L hrs being loaded in vehicle Park. 2 to HCoys equipment | |
| | 9-8-19 | | 3 Coys paraded at DUREN 13.44. All remaining horses of Division left 06.30 hrs for 24 Vety HP COLOGNE | |

Army Form C. 2118.

# WAR DIARY
## or
## INTELLIGENCE SUMMARY.
(Erase heading not required.) (Page 2)

Headquarters Highland Divisional Train

Instructions regarding War Diaries and Intelligence Summaries are contained in F.S. Regs., Part II. and the Staff Manual respectively. Title pages will be prepared in manuscript.

| Place | Date | Hour | Summary of Events and Information | Remarks and references to Appendices |
|---|---|---|---|---|
| DUREN | 10-8-19 | | Train HQ office closed & being loaded and defaulters personnel and baggage taken to DUREN Stn in train. Left DUREN Stn in train. | C&M |
| On rail. | 11-8-19 | | Halted at HUY 20.15 to 21.15 for men's meal. Halted for breakfast at GHISLENGHIEN about 0700. Detrained and happy and drink to order with guard, by train. N&S and 2 camp | C&M |
| CALAIS | 12-8-19 | | Arrived off 0915 hrs and entrained 0915. Train handed in and left CALAIS 1000 hrs for FOLKESTONE. Arrived CALAIS 1800 hrs. Accommodated | C&M |

C. M. Murri Capt. + Adj
LIEUT. COLONEL,
COMMDG HIGHLAND DIVISIONAL TRAIN.

www.ingramcontent.com/pod-product-compliance
Lightning Source LLC
Chambersburg PA
CBHW081405160426
43193CB00013B/2108